国际教育·海外考试·综合英语

出国英语标化考试词汇，一本就够！

出国考试词汇一本通

Examination For Study Abroad

朗阁东方教研组 组编

赵白 编著

基础

U0139832

机械工业出版社
CHINA MACHINE PRESS

对于大多数学生来说，基础词汇具备非常大的共通性。本书专为准备出国考试的学生设计，旨在根据 CEFR（Common European Framework of Reference for Languages，欧洲语言共同参考框架）标准，以一本通的形式对各考试中的常见单词进行总结归纳，除单词的释义、例句之外，每个单词下还标注了该词曾在哪些考试中出现过。本书的设计初衷是在一本书内尽可能囊括学生需要的内容，解决学生在不同考试之间横跨时的障碍，减少选择参考书的成本。

这本单词书既可以用作出国考试准备资料，也可以用作应对各类英语等级考试的辅助材料。

图书在版编目（CIP）数据

出国考试词汇一本通. 基础／赵白编著. —北京：
机械工业出版社，2023.11
ISBN 978 - 7 - 111 - 74328 - 6

Ⅰ.①出…　Ⅱ.①赵…　Ⅲ.①英语-词汇-自学参考
资料　Ⅳ.①H313

中国国家版本馆 CIP 数据核字（2023）第 225856 号

机械工业出版社（北京市百万庄大街 22 号　邮政编码 100037）
策划编辑：孙铁军　　责任编辑：孙铁军　尹小云
责任校对：张晓娟　　责任印制：张　博
北京联兴盛业印刷股份有限公司印刷
2024 年 1 月第 1 版第 1 次印刷
148mm×210mm・9.75 印张・297 千字
标准书号：ISBN 978 - 7 - 111 - 74328 - 6
定价：52.80 元

电话服务　　　　　　　　　网络服务
客服电话：010 - 88361066　　机 工 官 网：www.cmpbook.com
　　　　　010 - 88379833　　机 工 官 博：weibo.com/cmp1952
　　　　　010 - 68326294　　金 书 网：www.golden-book.com
封底无防伪标均为盗版　机工教育服务网：www.cmpedu.com

前　言

在过去十多年的教学生涯中，我参加过各种英语等级测试，也购买了大量的参考书。学英语必然要求背单词，而在浏览过书架上几十本单词参考书后，我发现其中大多数大同小异，雅思和托福的基础单词并没有本质上的不同。而在过去几年里，很多学生需要参加的考试更是多种多样，他们经常会从一个考试转到另一个考试，也经常为购买哪一本单词书而烦恼。

作为一名专业的从业者，我在 2010 年前后就开始研究对标 CEFR 的教材及教学体系，但很有意思的是，至今为止国内的传统教材并未对标英语原生的一些等级标准，而常见的英语考试在成绩单上都有 A1、A2、B1、B2、C1 和 C2 这六个非常明确的标准体系，一些常见的水平考试现在甚至已经直接以 CEFR 标准命名。在这样一个大前提下，我便萌生了编写这本单词书的想法。与其给同样的单词牵强分类，非要分出哪个是听、说、读、写的必备词，不如对每个单词进行标注，按照考试的常用程度和各学科的出现频率进行分类，在一本书内尽可能囊括学生需要的内容。这样也能解决学生在不同考试之间横跨时的障碍，为学生减少选择参考书的成本。毕竟，语言学习除了考试之外，更多的是处理具体场景下的具体问题，小到推开门走进面包店，大到在医院和警局寻求帮助，解决这些具体的场景问题都要求学生具备相对准确的词汇积累。而很多出国考试的听力、口语中都会出现这些场景，因此将词汇按照出现频率进行分类，考生可以针对不同考试的科目进行专项记忆，会更有效率。

当然，在每个单词后面我都选择了一些从考试内容中摘选出来的例句，让学生在背单词的同时能掌握一些用法上的拓展和实用的内容。如果学生背单词时觉得太枯燥了，就读一读例句，感受一下单词在原句中的含义及用法，说不定会有更多的收获和体会。

最后，祝每一位学子学习顺利，早日考取自己想要的成绩。

编者

目 录

前 言

A

abandon

抛弃；放弃

vt. [əˈbændən]

考试 TOEFL/IELTS/PTE
科目 reading

Snow forced many drivers to abandon their vehicles.

大雪迫使许多司机弃车步行。

abnormal

变态的，反常的

adj. [æbˈnɔːml]

考试 TOEFL/IELTS/PTE
科目 listening

It's not known how many U. S. children have abnormal cholesterol.

不知道有多少美国孩子的胆固醇异常。

absence

缺乏，不存在；缺席，不在

n. [ˈæbsəns]

考试 KET/PET/IELTS/TOEFL/
PTE
科目 all

The case was dismissed in the absence of any definite proof.

因缺乏确凿证据，此案被驳回。

absorb

吸收；吸引……的注意；使全神贯注

vt. [əbˈsɔːb]

考试 TOEFL/IELTS/PTE
科目 reading

The surrounding small towns have been absorbed into the city.

四周的小城镇已被并入这座城市。

abstract

抽象的

adj. ［ˈæbstrækt］

考试 TOEFL/IELTS/PTE
科目 reading

The research showed that pre-school children are capable of thinking in abstract terms.
研究表明，学龄前儿童具有抽象思维的能力。

accept

接受，领受；认可，同意

vt. ［əkˈsept］

考试 KET/PET/IELTS/TOEFL/PTE
科目 all

The college he applied to has accepted him.
他申请的那所大学录取了他。

accessible

可接近的

adj. ［əkˈsesəbl］

考试 TOEFL/IELTS/PTE
科目 listening

The Center is easily accessible to the general public.
该中心普通大众可随意进入。

accommodate

提供住宿；使适应；容纳

vt. ［əˈkɒmədeɪt］

考试 TOEFL/IELTS/PTE
科目 listening

Students are accommodated in homes nearby.
学生们被安置在附近的住家中。

accomplish

完成；实现

vt. ［əˈkʌmplɪʃ］

考试 TOEFL/IELTS/PTE
科目 reading

If we'd all work together, I think we could accomplish our goal.
只要大家齐心协力，我想我们就能实现目标。

accumulate

积累，积聚

v. [əˈkjuːmjəleɪt]

考试 TOEFL/IELTS/PTE
科目 reading

Households accumulate wealth across a broad spectrum of assets.

家庭在以各种各样的资产形式积累财富。

accurate

正确无误的；准确的，精确的

adj. [ˈækjərət]

考试 TOEFL/IELTS/PTE
科目 listening

Police have stressed that this is the most accurate description of the killer to date.

警方强调这是迄今为止对凶手最精确的描述。

accustom

使习惯

vt. [əˈkʌstəm]

考试 KET/PET/IELTS/TOEFL/PTE
科目 listening

He had to accustom himself to the cold weather.

他不得不让自己适应寒冷的天气。

ache

疼痛；渴望

vi. [eɪk]

考试 KET/PET/IELTS/TOEFL/PTE
科目 all

My leg still aches when I sit down.

坐下时我的腿还会痛。

（身体某部位的）疼痛

n. [eɪk]

考试 KET/PET/IELTS/TOEFL/PTE
科目 all

Poor posture can cause neck ache, headaches and breathing problems.

姿势不当会导致颈部疼痛、头痛和呼吸困难。

aching

疼痛的

adj. ['eɪkɪŋ]

考试 KET/PET/IELTS/TOEFL/PTE
科目 all

The weary walkers soothed their aching feet in the sea.

走累了的人们把脚浸在海水中以缓解疼痛。

achievement

完成；成就，成绩

n. [ə'tʃiːvmənt]

考试 KET/PET/IELTS/TOEFL/PTE
科目 all

Reaching this agreement so quickly was a great achievement.

如此快速达成这项协定是一大伟绩。

acknowledge

承认；告知收悉；（公开）感谢

vt. [ək'nɒlɪdʒ]

考试 TOEFL/IELTS/PTE
科目 listening

He is widely acknowledged as the best player in the world. 他被公认为是全球最佳球员。

acquire

获得，取得

vt. [ə'kwaɪə(r)]

考试 TOEFL/IELTS/PTE
科目 reading

He has acquired a reputation as this country's premier solo violinist.

他已经赢得了该国首席小提琴独奏家的名誉。

act

扮演；行动；充当，起作用

v. [ækt]

考试 KET/PET/IELTS/TOEFL/PTE
科目 all

He acted both as the ship's surgeon and as chaplain for the men.

他在船上兼任水手们的外科医生和牧师。

行为；法令；（戏剧、歌剧等的）一幕

n. ［ækt］

考试 KET/PET/IELTS/TOEFL/
PTE
科目 all

Language interpretation is the whole point of the act of reading.

语言诠释是阅读行为的全部意义。

action

行为，动作；作用；运转；行动；战斗

n. ［ˈækʃn］

考试 KET/PET/IELTS/TOEFL/
PTE
科目 all

The time has come for action if these beautiful animals are to survive.

若要使这些美丽的动物能生存下去，现在就要行动起来。

active

活跃的；敏捷的；积极的；起作用的

adj. ［ˈæktɪv］

考试 KET/PET/IELTS/TOEFL/
PTE
科目 all

Companies need to take active steps to increase exports.

各公司需要采取积极措施增加出口。

activity

活动；活力

n. ［ækˈtɪvəti］

考试 KET/PET/IELTS/TOEFL/
PTE
科目 all

Their brain activity totally changed.

他们的大脑活动完全变了。

actor

男演员；演员；行动者

n. ［ˈæktə(r)］

考试 KET/PET/IELTS/TOEFL/
PTE
科目 all

You have to be a very good actor to play that part.

要想演那个角色，你必须是一名非常出色的演员。

actress

女演员

n. ［ˈæktrəs］

考试 KET/PET/IELTS/TOEFL/PTE
科目 all

She's a very great dramatic actress.
她是一位非常了不起的戏剧演员。

adapt

使适应；改编

vt. ［əˈdæpt］

考试 TOEFL/IELTS/PTE
科目 reading

The world will be different, and we will have to be prepared to adapt to the change.
世界会变得不同，我们必须做好准备以适应其变化。

add

加；增加（进）；补充说

vt. ［æd］

考试 KET/PET/IELTS/TOEFL/PTE
科目 all

Banks add all the interest and other charges together.
银行合计所有利息和其他费用。

address

住址；演说，演讲

n. ［əˈdres］

考试 KET/PET/IELTS/TOEFL/PTE
科目 all

We require details of your name and address.
我们需要你的姓名和地址的详细信息。

演说，演讲；写收信人姓名地址

vt. ［əˈdres］

考试 KET/PET/IELTS/TOEFL/PTE
科目 all

He is due to address a conference on human rights next week.
他下星期将在一次大会上发表关于人权的演说。

adequate

充分的，足够的；可胜任的，合格的

adj. [ˈædɪkwət]

考试 TOEFL/IELTS/PTE
科目 listening

The old methods weren't adequate to meet current needs.

老方法已不足以满足当前的需求。

adjust

校准，调整；适应，习惯

vt. [əˈdʒʌst]

考试 TOEFL/IELTS/PTE
科目 reading

We have been preparing our fighters to adjust themselves to civil society.

我们一直在培训我们的战士，以使他们适应普通的社会生活。

admit

承认；供认；准许……进入；准许……加入

vt. [ədˈmɪt]

考试 TOEFL/IELTS/PTE
科目 reading

Each ticket admits one adult and one child.

每张票可供一个成人和一个小孩入内。

adolescent

青少年

n. [ˌædəˈlesnt]

考试 TOEFL/IELTS/PTE
科目 reading

Young adolescents are happiest with small groups of close friends.

青少年在和自己小圈子里的好友待在一起时最开心。

adorn

装饰，装扮

vt. [əˈdɔːn]

考试 TOEFL/IELTS
科目 writing

Use seasonal flowers to adorn your Christmas tree.

你可以使用应季的花卉来装饰圣诞树。

adult

成年人

n. [ˈædʌlt]

考试 KET/PET/IELTS/TOEFL/ PTE
科目 all

Children must be accompanied by an adult.
儿童必须有成年人陪同。

advanced

超前的，先进的；高级的；（发展）晚期的

adj. [ədˈvɑːnst]

考试 TOEFL/IELTS/PTE
科目 reading

Without more training or advanced technical skills, they'll lose their jobs.
没有进一步的培训或高级技能的话，他们就会丢掉工作。

advantage

优点，长处；有利条件；利益，好处

n. [ədˈvɑːntɪdʒ]

考试 KET/PET/IELTS/TOEFL/ PTE
科目 all

The great advantage of home-grown oranges is their magnificent flavour.
家产柑橘的一大好处是口感极佳。

advertisement

广告；公告；广告宣传

n. [ədˈvɜːtɪsmənt]

考试 KET/PET/IELTS/TOEFL/ PTE
科目 all

She recently placed an advertisement in the local newspaper.
她最近在本地报纸上登了一则广告。

advice

劝告，忠告；意见，建议

n. [ədˈvaɪs]

考试 KET/PET/IELTS/TOEFL/ PTE
科目 all

Take my advice and stay away from him!
听我的，离他远远的！

advocate

倡导者；辩护人

n. [ˈædvəkət]

考试 TOEFL/IELTS/PTE
科目 listening

He was a strong advocate of free market policies and a multi-party system.

他是自由市场政策和多党派制度的坚定拥护者。

afford

付得起；供给

vt. [əˈfɔːd]

考试 KET/PET/IELTS/TOEFL/
PTE
科目 all

We couldn't afford to buy a new rug.

我们买不起新的小地毯。

afraid

害怕的，恐惧的；犯愁的，不乐意的

adj. [əˈfreɪd]

考试 KET/PET/IELTS/TOEFL/
PTE
科目 all

I'm still afraid to sleep in my own bedroom.

我还是不敢在自己的卧室里睡觉。

agent

代理人，代理商；产生作用的人或事物

n. [ˈeɪdʒənt]

考试 KET/PET/IELTS/TOEFL/
PTE
科目 all

You are buying direct, rather than through an agent.

你这是直接购买，不是通过代理人购买。

aggressive

侵略的；挑衅的；志在必得的；积极进取的

adj. [əˈgresɪv]

考试 KET/PET/IELTS/TOEFL/
PTE
科目 all

A good salesperson has to be aggressive in today's competitive market.

在当今竞争激烈的市场上，一名优秀的销售人员应该具有进取精神。

aid

援助；救援物资；助手；辅助物

n. ［eɪd］

考试 KET/PET/IELTS/TOEFL/ PTE
科目 all

They have already pledged billions of dollars in aid.
他们已经许诺援助几十亿美元。

援助，帮助

v. ［eɪd］

考试 KET/PET/IELTS/TOEFL/ PTE
科目 all

The hunt for her killer will continue, with police aided by the army and air force.
在陆军和空军的帮助下，警方将继续追踪谋杀她的凶手。

aim

目的，目标；瞄准

n. ［eɪm］

考试 KET/PET/IELTS/TOEFL/ PTE
科目 all

Teamwork is required in order to achieve the aims.
要想达到这些目标，需要齐心协力。

目的是；旨在

vi. ［eɪm］

考试 KET/PET/IELTS/TOEFL/ PTE
科目 all

The new measures are aimed at tightening existing sanctions.
新措施旨在加强现行的制裁。

airway

(飞机的) 固定航线

n. ［ˈeəˌweɪ］

考试 KET/PET/IELTS/TOEFL/ PTE
科目 all

How does a private pilot get access to the airways?
私人飞行员如何进入固定航线呢?

alarm

警报；惊慌

n. [əˈlɑːm]

考试 KET/PET/IELTS/TOEFL/
PTE
科目 all

The doctor said there was no cause of alarm.

医生说不必惊慌。

使忧虑；使惊恐

vt. [əˈlɑːm]

考试 KET/PET/IELTS/TOEFL/
PTE
科目 all

We could not see what had alarmed him.

我们不清楚是什么使他忧虑不安。

---

alert

机警的，警觉的；戒备的

adj. [əˈlɜːt]

考试 TOEFL/IELTS/PTE
科目 reading

We all have to stay alert.

我们都必须保持警惕。

---

alienate

使疏远；离间；使（与某群体）格格不入

vt. [ˈeɪliəneɪt]

考试 TOEFL/IELTS
科目 writing

Very talented children may feel alienated from the others in their class.

天资出众的孩子可能会感觉与班里的其他人格格不入。

---

allot

分配，配给；分派（任务等）

vt. [əˈlɒt]

考试 TOEFL/IELTS
科目 writing

We were allotted half an hour to address the committee.

我们被给予半小时向委员会做陈述。

allow

允许，准许；承认；给予

vt. [əˈlaʊ]

考试 KET/PET/IELTS/TOEFL/PTE
科目 all

The Government will allow them to advertise on radio and television.
政府将准许他们在广播和电视上做广告。

alter

改变，更改；修改（衣服使更合身）

v. [ˈɔːltə(r)]

考试 TOEFL/IELTS
科目 writing

The old landscape has been radically altered, severely damaging wildlife.
原有的景观已彻底变了样，严重损害了野生动植物。

alternative

可供选择的事物

n. [ɔːlˈtɜːnətɪv]

考试 TOEFL/IELTS/PTE
科目 listening

New ways to treat arthritis may provide an alternative to painkillers.
关节炎的新疗法可能是止痛药之外的另一种选择。

amaze

使惊奇

vt. [əˈmeɪz]

考试 KET/PET/IELTS/TOEFL/PTE
科目 all

Show this video to Dad on his special day and amaze him.
在父亲节那天让父亲看这段录像，给他一个惊喜。

ambitious

有抱负的，雄心勃勃的；有野心的

adj. [æmˈbɪʃəs]

考试 TOEFL/IELTS/PTE
科目 reading

Mike is so ambitious, so determined to do it all.
麦克踌躇满志，决心要将它都做完。

amount

总计，共计

vi. [ə'maʊnt]

考试 KET/PET/IELTS/TOEFL/PTE
科目 all

The bill amounts to $102.
此账单共计 102 美元。

金额；数量，数额

n. [ə'maʊnt]

考试 KET/PET/IELTS/TOEFL/PTE
科目 all

The insurance company will refund any amount due to you.
保险公司将赔偿你应得的所有款项。

analysis

分析；分解

n. [ə'næləsɪs]

考试 KET/PET/IELTS/TOEFL/PTE
科目 all

The blood samples are sent to the laboratory for analysis.
血样要送到实验室进行分析。

analyze

分析，分解

vt. ['ænəlaɪz]

考试 TOEFL/IELTS/PTE
科目 listening

The job involves gathering and analyzing data.
这项工作包括搜集和分析资料。

anger

愤怒，气愤

n. ['æŋgə(r)]

考试 KET/PET/IELTS/TOEFL/PTE
科目 all

He cried with anger and frustration.
他愤怒而又沮丧地哭了起来。

使发怒，激怒；发怒

v. ['æŋgə(r)]

考试 KET/PET/IELTS/TOEFL/
PTE
科目 all

The question clearly angered him.

这个问题显然激怒了他。

He angers with little provocation.

他受点小刺激就会发怒。

angle

角，角度

n. ['æŋgl]

考试 KET/PET/IELTS/TOEFL/
PTE
科目 all

The boat is now leaning at a 30 degree angle.

这艘船正以 30 度角倾斜。

钓鱼；（采用各种方法）取得；斜移，斜置

v. ['æŋgl]

考试 KET/PET/IELTS/TOEFL/
PTE
科目 all

It sounds as if he's just angling for sympathy.

听起来他似乎只是在博取同情。

animate

使有活力，激活

vt. ['ænɪmeɪt]

考试 TOEFL/IELTS
科目 writing

Environmental issues animate the conversation on microblog.

有关环境的问题推动了微博上的对话。

announce

宣布，宣称；通知；广播（电台节目等）

vt. [ə'naʊns]

考试 KET/PET/IELTS/TOEFL/
PTE
科目 all

He will announce tonight that he is resigning from office.

他将于今晚宣布辞职。

announcement

通知；宣布；通告

n. [əˈnaʊnsmənt]

考试 KET/PET/IELTS/TOEFL/
PTE
科目 all

There has been no formal announcement by either government.

双方政府都未发出正式通告。

annual

每年的，年度的；一年的

adj. [ˈænjuəl]

考试 TOEFL/IELTS/PTE
科目 reading

In its annual report, UNICEF says at least 40,000 children die every day.

在其年度报告中，联合国儿童基金会称每天至少有四万名儿童死亡。

anticipate

预料；期望；预先考虑；抢先

vt. [ænˈtɪsɪpeɪt]

考试 TOEFL/IELTS/PTE
科目 listening

It is anticipated that inflation will stabilize at 3%.

据预测，通货膨胀将稳定在3%。

anxiety

忧虑；渴望

n. [æŋˈzaɪəti]

考试 KET/PET/IELTS/TOEFL/
PTE
科目 all

If you're worried about your health, share your anxieties with your doctor.

你要是担心自己的健康状况，就把你的忧虑告诉医生吧。

anxious

焦虑的，担心的；急于（得到的），渴望的

adj. [ˈæŋkʃəs]

考试 KET/PET/IELTS/TOEFL/
PTE
科目 all

There are plenty of graduates anxious for work.

大量的毕业生渴望得到工作。

anxiously

焦急地；急切地

adv. [ˈæŋkʃəsli]

考试 KET/PET/IELTS/TOEFL/PTE
科目 all

They are waiting anxiously to see who will succeed him.

他们焦急地等待着看谁会接替他。

apologize

道歉，认错

vi. [əˈpɒlədʒaɪz]

考试 KET/PET/IELTS/TOEFL/PTE
科目 all

We apologize for the late departure of this flight.

本次航班延误离境，谨致歉意。

apology

道歉，认错

n. [əˈpɒlədʒi]

考试 KET/PET/IELTS/TOEFL/PTE
科目 all

We received a letter of apology.

我们收到了一封致歉信。

apparent

明显的；表面上的

adj. [əˈpærənt]

考试 TOEFL/IELTS/PTE
科目 listening

For no apparent reason, the train suddenly stopped.

不知什么原因，火车突然停了下来。

appear

出现；出场；问世；仿佛；出版

vi. [əˈpɪə(r)]

考试 KET/PET/IELTS/TOEFL/PTE
科目 all

A woman appeared at the far end of the street.

一个女人远远出现在街道的尽头。

appearance

出现，露面；外表；公开露面

n. ［ə'pɪərəns］

考试 KET/PET/IELTS/TOEFL/
PTE
科目 all

It was the president's second public appearance to date.

这是总统到那时为止的第二次公开露面。

applaud

鼓掌欢迎；赞成

v. ［ə'plɔːd］

考试 TOEFL/IELTS
科目 writing

The audience laughed and applauded.

观众边笑边鼓掌。

applicable

可应用（实施）的；适当的，合适的

adj. ［ə'plɪkəbl］

考试 TOEFL/IELTS/PTE
科目 reading

What is a reasonable standard for one family is not applicable for another.

对一个家庭合理的标准并不适用于另一个家庭。

applicant

申请人，申请者

n. ［'æplɪkənt］

考试 TOEFL/IELTS/PTE
科目 reading

The goal of the task was to hire the best applicant in a simulated job search.

这项任务的目标是在模拟找工作的环节中雇用最合适的申请人。

application

申请，请求；申请表，申请书；应用，运用

n. ［ˌæplɪ'keɪʃn］

考试 KET/PET/IELTS/TOEFL/
PTE
科目 all

Applications should be submitted as early as possible.

申请表应尽早提交。

appoint

任命，委派；指定；约定（时间、地点等）

vt. [əˈpɔɪnt]

考试 KET/PET/IELTS/TOEFL/PTE
科目 all

The Prime Minister has appointed a civilian as defence minister.
首相已委任一位平民为国防部长。

appointment

约会；职位

n. [əˈpɔɪntmənt]

考试 KET/PET/IELTS/TOEFL/PTE
科目 all

She has an appointment with her accountant.
她和她的会计约好了见面。

appreciate

感激，感谢；欣赏，赏识；理解，领会

vt. [əˈpriːʃieɪt]

考试 TOEFL/IELTS/PTE
科目 listening

I'd appreciate it if you wouldn't mention it.
如果你不提它，我会很感激。

approach

接近；着手处理

v. [əˈprəʊtʃ]

考试 TOEFL/IELTS/PTE
科目 reading

As you approach the town, you'll see the college on the left.
快到市镇时，你就可以看到左边的学院。

appropriate

合适的

adj. [əˈprəʊpriət]

考试 TOEFL/IELTS/PTE
科目 reading

The book was written in a style appropriate to the age of the children.
这本书的文体适合儿童阅读。

approximately

近似地，大约

adv. ［ə'prɒksɪmətli］

考试 TOEFL/IELTS/PTE
科目 listening

Approximately $150 million is to be spent on improvements.
大约 1.5 亿美元将用于改善工作。

architecture

建筑；建筑学；建筑式样或风格；建筑物

n. ［'ɑːkɪtektʃə(r)］

考试 TOEFL/IELTS/PTE
科目 listening

He studied classical architecture and design in Rome.
他在罗马学习了古典建筑学和设计。

arrow

箭，矢；箭状物；箭头符号

n. ［'ærəʊ］

考试 KET/PET/IELTS/TOEFL/
PTE
科目 all

Warriors armed with bows, arrows and spears have invaded villages.
携带弓箭和长矛的武士们闯入了村庄。

artist

艺术家；（尤指）画家；专业演员，艺人

n. ［'ɑːtɪst］

考试 KET/PET/IELTS/TOEFL/
PTE
科目 all

His books are enormously easy to read, yet he is a serious artist.
虽然他是一名不折不扣的艺术家，但是他写的书极其通俗易懂。

artistic

艺术（家）的；有美术才能的；有艺术天赋的

adj. ［ɑː'tɪstɪk］

考试 KET/PET/IELTS/TOEFL/
PTE
科目 all

Her natural creativity and artistic talent make her home a real showstopper.
她天生的创造力和艺术天赋让她的家不同凡响，令人叹服。

aspect

样子，外表，面貌；（问题等的）方面

n. ['æspekt]

考试 TOEFL/IELTS/PTE
科目 listening

Our journey had taken on a new aspect. The countryside was no longer familiar.

我们所到之地呈现出一派新景象。乡村变得不再熟悉。

assemble

聚集；装配

v. [ə'sembl]

考试 TOEFL/IELTS/PTE
科目 reading

He has assembled a team of experts to handle queries.

他召集了一批专家来答疑解惑。

assess

评价；估值

vt. [ə'ses]

考试 TOEFL/IELTS/PTE
科目 listening

The test was to assess aptitude rather than academic achievement.

这次测试是考查能力，而不是学习成绩。

assign

分配；确定时间或地点；指派

vt. [ə'saɪn]

考试 TOEFL/IELTS/PTE
科目 listening

The teacher assigned each of the children a different task.

老师给每个孩子布置了不同的作业。

assignment

分配，指派；（指定的）作业；（分派的）任务

n. [ə'saɪnmənt]

考试 TOEFL/IELTS/PTE
科目 reading

The assessment for the course involves written assignments and practical tests.

这门课程的考核包括书面作业和实际操作考试。

assist

协助，帮助；促进

vt. ［ə'sɪst］

考试 TOEFL/IELTS/PTE
科目 reading

Julia was assisting him to prepare his speech.

朱莉娅正在帮他准备演讲稿。

assistant

助理的，副的

adj. ［ə'sɪstənt］

考试 KET/PET/IELTS/TOEFL/PTE
科目 all

He is a young assistant professor at Harvard.

他是哈佛大学的一名年轻副教授。

助手；助教

n. ［ə'sɪstənt］

考试 KET/PET/IELTS/TOEFL/PTE
科目 all

The salesman has been accompanied to the meeting by an assistant.

营销人员在助手的陪同下参加了会议。

association

联盟，协会，社团；交往；联合；联想

n. ［ə,səʊʃi'eɪʃn］

考试 KET/PET/IELTS/TOEFL/PTE
科目 all

Research associations are often linked to a particular industry.

研究协会通常与某个特定的行业挂钩。

assume

假定；承担；呈现；装出

vt. ［ə'sjuːm］

考试 TOEFL/IELTS/PTE
科目 reading

If the package is wrapped well, we assume the contents are also wonderful.

如果包装精美，我们就会认为里面装的也是好东西。

astound

使惊讶

vt. [əˈstaʊnd]

考试 TOEFL/IELTS
科目 writing

He used to astound his friends with feats of physical endurance.

过去，他表现出来的惊人耐力常让朋友们大吃一惊。

astronaut

宇航员，航天员

n. [ˈæstrənɔːt]

考试 KET/PET/IELTS/TOEFL/PTE
科目 all

In some spots, decades-old astronaut footprints are still visible.

在一些地点，几十年前老宇航员的脚印依然可见。

athlete

运动员；擅长运动的人

n. [ˈæθliːt]

考试 KET/PET/IELTS/TOEFL/PTE
科目 all

As an athlete, he was a late starter.

作为一名运动员，他起步已晚。

athletic

田径运动的，体育运动的；健壮的

adj. [æθˈletɪk]

考试 KET/PET/IELTS/TOEFL/PTE
科目 all

Most athletic activities are about individual effort.

大多数体育项目是靠个人的拼搏。

Atlantic

大西洋的

adj. [ætˈlæntɪk]

考试 KET/PET/IELTS/TOEFL/PTE
科目 all

They consider the Arctic Ocean a northern part of the Atlantic Ocean.

他们将北冰洋看作是大西洋的北部。

大西洋

n. ［æt'læntɪk］

考试 KET/PET/IELTS/TOEFL/
PTE
科目 all

Nor has the plan won overwhelming support across the Atlantic .

这项计划在大西洋的对岸没有得到普遍的支持。

attach

系上，附上；重视；与……有关联

v. ［ə'tætʃ］

考试 TOEFL/IELTS/PTE
科目 reading

We attach labels to things before we file them away.

存档前，我们先在物品上贴上标签。

attack

攻击；抨击，非难；（疾病）发作，侵袭

n. ［ə'tæk］

考试 KET/PET/IELTS/TOEFL/
PTE
科目 all

They claimed responsibility for the attack .

他们宣称对这起袭击负责。

攻击；抨击，非难；侵袭，损害；进攻

v. ［ə'tæk］

考试 KET/PET/IELTS/TOEFL/
PTE
科目 all

A newspaper ran an editorial attacking him for being a showman.

一家报纸发表社论，批评他善于作秀。

attain

获得；达到

vt. ［ə'teɪn］

考试 TOEFL/IELTS
科目 writing

Jim is halfway to attaining his pilot's licence.

吉姆就快要拿到飞行员执照了。

attempt

尝试，企图

vt. ［ə'tempt］

考试 TOEFL/IELTS/PTE
科目 listening

I don't want to attempt anything too fancy.
我不想尝试那些过于花哨的事情。

attend

出席，参加；注意，专心；随同，陪同

v. ［ə'tend］

考试 KET/PET/IELTS/TOEFL/
PTE
科目 all

Thousands of people attended the funeral.
数千人参加了葬礼。
I have some urgent business to attend to.
我有一些急事要处理。

attitude

态度，看法；姿势

n. ［'ætɪtjuːd］

考试 TOEFL/IELTS/PTE
科目 listening

Being unemployed produces negative attitudes to work.
失业会导致对工作的消极态度。

attract

引起注意（或兴趣等）；吸引；激起

vt. ［ə'trækt］

考试 KET/PET/IELTS/TOEFL/
PTE
科目 all

Summer attracts visitors to the countryside.
在夏季，乡村游很吸引游客。

attraction

吸引；吸引力；引力；向往的地方；有吸引力的事

n. ［ə'trækʃn］

考试 KET/PET/IELTS/TOEFL/
PTE
科目 all

There's the added attraction of free champagne on all flights.
所有的航班机都免费供应香槟，这是额外的吸引力

attribute

归因于

vt. [əˈtrɪbjuːt]

考试 TOEFL/IELTS/PTE
科目 reading

Women tend to attribute their success to external causes such as luck.

女性倾向于将她们的成功归因于外部因素，比如运气。

audience

听众，观众；读者

n. [ˈɔːdiəns]

考试 TOEFL/IELTS/PTE
科目 listening

The entire audience broke into loud applause.

全场观众爆发出热烈的掌声。

author

作者，作家，著作人；创造者，发起人

n. [ˈɔːθə(r)]

考试 KET/PET/IELTS/TOEFL/
PTE
科目 all

He is Japan's best-selling author.

他是日本的畅销书作家。

authority

权力；威信；当局；权威

n. [ɔːˈθɒrəti]

考试 KET/PET/IELTS/TOEFL/
PTE
科目 all

The health authorities are investigating the problem.

卫生当局正在调查这个问题。

authorize

授权，批准

vt. [ˈɔːθəraɪz]

考试 TOEFL/IELTS
科目 writing

We are willing to authorize the president to use force if necessary.

我们愿意授权总统在必要的时候使用武力。

automatic

自动的；无意识的

adj. [ˌɔːtəˈmætɪk]

考试 KET/PET/IELTS/TOEFL/PTE
科目 all

Breathing is an automatic function of the body.
呼吸是身体的一种无意识的功能。

avail

有益于，有用

v. [əˈveɪl]

考试 TOEFL/IELTS
科目 writing

Guests are encouraged to avail themselves of the full range of hotel facilities.
旅馆鼓励客人充分利用各种设施。

availability

有效（性）；可得性

n. [əˌveɪləˈbɪləti]

考试 TOEFL/IELTS/PTE
科目 reading

Before travelling we must ensure the availability of petrol and oil.
旅行前，我们必须确保能够买到汽油和机油。

available

可获得的，可用的；有空的

adj. [əˈveɪləbl]

考试 TOEFL/IELTS/PTE
科目 listening

There are three small boats available for hire.
有 3 艘小船可供出租。

avenue

林荫道，大街；（比喻）途径，手段，方法

n. [ˈævənjuː]

考试 KET/PET/IELTS/TOEFL/PTE
科目 all

We will explore every avenue until we find an answer.
我们要探索一切途径，直到找到答案为止。

average

平均，平均数

n. [ˈævərɪdʒ]

考试 KET/PET/IELTS/TOEFL/ PTE
科目 all

Parents spend an average of $220 a year on toys for their children.

父母给孩子买玩具的花费每年平均为 220 美元。

平均的；普通的

adj. [ˈævərɪdʒ]

考试 KET/PET/IELTS/TOEFL/ PTE
科目 all

The average price of goods rose by just 2.2%.

商品平均价格仅上涨了 2.2%。

平均为；计算出……的平均数

v. [ˈævərɪdʒ]

考试 KET/PET/IELTS/TOEFL/ PTE
科目 all

The cost should average out at about $6 per person.

费用应该是平均每人约六美元。

avoid

避免，逃避

vt. [əˈvɔɪd]

考试 KET/PET/IELTS/TOEFL/ PTE
科目 all

The pilots had to take emergency action to avoid a disaster.

飞行员不得不采取紧急措施避免灾难的发生。

award

授予，奖给

vt. [əˈwɔːd]

考试 KET/PET/IELTS/TOEFL/ PTE
科目 all

She was awarded the prize for both films.

她的两部电影双双获奖。

奖，奖金；(赔偿) 裁决；授予

n. [ə'wɔːd]

考试 KET/PET/IELTS/TOEFL/PTE
科目 all

The novel won the 1964 national book award for fiction.

这部小说在 1964 年获得了国家图书小说类奖。

aware

知道的，意识到的

adj. [ə'weə(r)]

考试 TOEFL/IELTS/PTE
科目 listening

Smokers are well aware of the dangers to their own health.

吸烟的人都很清楚吸烟对自身健康的危害。

awful

可怕的；糟糕的；极讨厌的；很多的，过多的

adj. ['ɔːfl]

考试 KET/PET/IELTS/TOEFL/PTE
科目 all

We met and I thought he was awful.

我们见了面，我觉得他很讨厌。

awkward

难处理的；笨拙的；令人尴尬的

adj. ['ɔːkwəd]

考试 TOEFL/IELTS/PTE
科目 listening

I was the first to ask him awkward questions but there'll be harder ones to come.

我是第一个向他提出尴尬问题的人，不过还会有人问更难回答的问题。

B

baby-sitter

看护小孩的人

n. [ˈbeɪbisɪtə(r)]

考试 KET/PET/IELTS/TOEFL/PTE
科目 all

Too many experts tell us that good mothers do not abandon their children to baby-sitters.

太多专家告诉我们，好母亲不会把孩子留给保姆。

backdate

回溯；倒填日期

vt. [ˌbækˈdeɪt]

考试 TOEFL/IELTS
科目 writing

The contract that was signed on Thursday morning was backdated to March 11.

周四早上签订的合同实际生效日期追溯到 3 月 11 日。

background

背景，经历；幕后

n. [ˈbækɡraʊnd]

考试 TOEFL/IELTS/PTE
科目 listening

The job would suit someone with a business background.

这份工作适合有商务经验的人。

badminton

羽毛球运动；羽毛球

n. [ˈbædmɪntən]

考试 KET/PET/IELTS/TOEFL/PTE
科目 all

The Badminton Club holds coaching sessions for beginners and intermediate players on Friday evenings.

羽毛球俱乐部每周五晚上为初学者与中等水平练习者开设训练课程。

baggage

行李

n. ['bægɪdʒ]

考试 KET/PET/IELTS/TOEFL/PTE
科目 all

The passengers went through immigration control and collected their baggage.
旅客通过入境检查后领取了自己的行李。

balance

平衡；天平；余额

n. ['bæləns]

考试 KET/PET/IELTS/TOEFL/PTE
科目 all

Tourists often disturb the delicate balance of nature on the island.
观光客常常破坏岛上微妙的自然生态平衡。

band

条，带；乐队；波段；一群，一伙

n. [bænd]

考试 KET/PET/IELTS/TOEFL/PTE
科目 all

Local bands provide music for dancing.
当地的乐队为跳舞伴乐。

bandage

绷带

n. ['bændɪdʒ]

考试 KET/PET/IELTS/TOEFL/PTE
科目 all

His chest was swathed in bandages.
他的胸部缠着绷带。

用绷带包扎

v. ['bændɪdʒ]

考试 KET/PET/IELTS/TOEFL/PTE
科目 all

His injured leg was all bandaged up.
他受伤的腿上缠满了绷带。

banker

银行家

n. [ˈbæŋkə(r)]

考试 KET/PET/IELTS/TOEFL/
PTE
科目 all

He was until very recently the most powerful banker in the city.

到最近为止，他一直都是这个城市里最有实力的银行家。

bar

棍；闩；酒吧；障碍；条；栏杆

n. [bɑː(r)]

考试 KET/PET/IELTS/TOEFL/
PTE
科目 all

All the ground floor windows were fitted with bars.

底层所有的窗户都安装了栅栏。

闩门；阻挡；排斥，不准

vt. [bɑː(r)]

考试 KET/PET/IELTS/TOEFL/
PTE
科目 all

Bar the barn door so the cows can't get out.

闩上牲口棚门以免牛跑出去。

barber

理发师

n. [ˈbɑːbə(r)]

考试 KET/PET/IELTS/TOEFL/
PTE
科目 all

The barber asked him about his trip to Rome.

理发师问他的罗马之行怎么样。

barrier

栅栏；屏障；障碍（物）

n. [ˈbæriə(r)]

考试 TOEFL/IELTS/PTE
科目 reading

The demonstrators broke through heavy police barriers.

示威者们冲破了警察的重重设防。

barter

货物交换；以物易物

v. [ˈbɑːtə(r)]

考试 TOEFL/IELTS
科目 writing

The local people have been bartering wheat for cotton and timber.
当地人一直用小麦交换棉花和木材。

baseball

棒球；棒球运动

n. [ˈbeɪsbɔːl]

考试 KET/PET/IELTS/TOEFL/PTE
科目 all

Baseball is America's favourite pastime.
棒球是美国人最喜欢的娱乐活动。

basic

基本的，基础的

adj. [ˈbeɪsɪk]

考试 KET/PET/IELTS/TOEFL/PTE
科目 all

The campsite provided only basic facilities.
野营地只提供基本的设施。

bat

球拍，球棒；短棒；蝙蝠

n. [bæt]

考试 KET/PET/IELTS/TOEFL/PTE
科目 all

The bat costs a dollar more than the ball.
球棒比球贵一美元。

bathe

浸到水中；游泳

v. [beɪð]

考试 TOEFL/IELTS
科目 writing

The police have warned the city's inhabitants not to bathe in the polluted river.
警方已经告诫该市居民不要在这条被污染的河里游泳。

bathroom

浴室；盥洗室，卫生间

n. [ˈbɑːθruːm]

考试 KET/PET/IELTS/TOEFL/ PTE
科目 all

The master bedroom has its own bathroom.
主卧室带有独立卫生间。

battery

电池（组）；一组，一群，一批

n. [ˈbætri]

考试 KET/PET/IELTS/TOEFL/ PTE
科目 all

The shavers come complete with batteries.
这些剃须刀已经配好了电池。

bay

海湾

n. [beɪ]

考试 KET/PET/IELTS/TOEFL/ PTE
科目 all

The ships in the bay present a beautiful sight.
海湾内的船只呈现出一派美丽的景象。

beach

海滩，湖滨，河滩

n. [biːtʃ]

考试 KET/PET/IELTS/TOEFL/ PTE
科目 all

I just want to lie on the beach in the sun.
我只想躺在海滩上晒晒太阳。

bean

豆；菜豆

n. [biːn]

考试 KET/PET/IELTS/TOEFL/ PTE
科目 all

Here are a few things we'd like to see in jelly bean.
这些是我们希望在果冻豆看到的东西。

beat

敲击（声）；心跳；节拍

n. [biːt]

考试 KET/PET/IELTS/TOEFL/ PTE
科目 all

He could hear the beat of his heart.
他能听到自己的心跳。

敲打；快速搅拌；胜过；心跳

v. ［biːt］

考试 KET/PET/IELTS/TOEFL/PTE
科目 all

Hailstones beat against the window.
冰雹砸在窗户上。

become

变成，开始变得；适合，与……相称

v. ［bɪˈkʌm］

考试 KET/PET/IELTS/TOEFL/PTE
科目 all

It soon became apparent that no one was going to come.
很快就很清楚，没人会来。
Such behaviour did not become her.
这种举止与她的身份不相称。

bedroom

卧室

n. ［ˈbedruːm］

考试 KET/PET/IELTS/TOEFL/PTE
科目 all

The table was painted to match the window frame in the bedroom.
这张桌子刷上了与卧室窗框相配的颜色。

beforehand

预先，事先

v. ［bɪˈfɔːhænd］

考试 KET/PET/IELTS/TOEFL/PTE
科目 all

Please inform me of your arrival time beforehand.
请事先通知我你抵达的时间。

beg

恳求，请求，乞求；行乞，乞讨

v. ［beg］

考试 KET/PET/IELTS/TOEFL/PTE
科目 all

I begged him to come back to England with me.
我恳求他和我一起回英格兰。
I was surrounded by people begging for food.
我被一群讨饭的围住了。

beginning

开始，开端；起源，早期阶段

n. [bɪˈɡɪnɪŋ]

考试 KET/PET/IELTS/TOEFL/
PTE
科目 all

This was the beginning of her recording career.
这是她灌制唱片生涯的开始。

behaviour

行为，举止；表现方式，活动方式

n. [bɪˈheɪvjə(r)]

考试 TOEFL/IELTS/PTE
科目 listening

A person's behaviour is often regulated by his circumstances.
人的行为常受其所处环境的约束。

behind

在……的后面，落后于；是……产生的原因

prep. [bɪˈhaɪnd]

考试 KET/PET/IELTS/TOEFL/
PTE
科目 all

He was the man behind the plan to build a new hospital.
他就是策划修建新医院的人。

belong

属于，附属，隶属；应归入（类别、范畴等）

vi. [bɪˈlɒŋ]

考试 KET/PET/IELTS/TOEFL/
PTE
科目 all

The house has belonged to her family for three or four generations.
这栋房子归她们家有三四代人了。

bench

长凳，长椅；（工作）台，座

n. [bentʃ]

考试 KET/PET/IELTS/TOEFL/
PTE
科目 all

He sat down on a park bench.
他坐在公园里的长椅上。

beneficial

有益的，有利的

adj. [ˌbenɪˈfɪʃl]

考试 TOEFL/IELTS/PTE
科目 listening

Using computers has a beneficial effect on children's learning.

使用计算机对孩子们的学习有益。

berry

浆果，莓

n. [ˈberi]

考试 KET/PET/IELTS/TOEFL/PTE
科目 all

You can find a local farm and go berry picking.

你可以找一个当地的农场去采浆果。

bet

打赌；敢断定

v. [bet]

考试 KET/PET/IELTS/TOEFL/PTE
科目 all

He bet them 500 pounds that they would lose.

他和他们打赌 500 英镑说他们会输。

打赌，赌注；预计，估计

n. [bet]

考试 TOEFL/IELTS/PTE
科目 listening

Clothes are a safe bet as a present for a teenager.

衣服适合作为送给十几岁孩子的礼物。

bill

账单；海报，招贴，议案，钞票

n. [bɪl]

考试 KET/PET/IELTS/TOEFL/PTE
科目 all

They couldn't afford to pay the bills.

他们无力支付这些账单。

开账单；把（某人或事物）宣传为……；宣布

vt. ［bɪl］

考试 KET/PET/IELTS/TOEFL/
PTE
科目 all

She was billed to play the Wicked Queen in *Snow White*.

她已被宣布将出演《白雪公主》里狠毒的王后。

biologist

生物学家

n. ［baɪˈɒlədʒɪst］

考试 KET/PET/IELTS/TOEFL/
PTE
科目 all

He is a leading marine biologist.

他是一位卓越的海洋生物学家。

biology

生物学；生理

n. ［baɪˈɒlədʒi］

考试 KET/PET/IELTS/TOEFL/
PTE
科目 all

The biology of these diseases is terribly complicated.

这些疾病的机理极其复杂。

bit

一点，一些；小块，少量；片刻

n. ［bɪt］

考试 KET/PET/IELTS/TOEFL/
PTE
科目 all

With a bit of luck, we'll be there by 12.

如果运气好的话，我们将于 12 点钟赶到那里。

bitter

有苦味的；辛酸的；怀恨的

adj. ［ˈbɪtə(r)］

考试 KET/PET/IELTS/TOEFL/
PTE
科目 all

There are different types of roots that you can get called the bitter and the sweet.

这些根有不同的类型，被称为苦的和甜的。

苦啤酒

n. ［'bɪtə(r)］

考试 KET/PET/IELTS/TOEFL/PTE
科目 all

There is a pint of bitter.

这儿有一品脱苦啤酒。

blank

没有写字的；空白的；无图画的；无表情的

adj. ［blæŋk］

考试 KET/PET/IELTS/TOEFL/PTE
科目 all

Sign your name in the blank space below.

把你的名字签在下面的空白处。

空白（处）；空虚；空弹

n. ［blæŋk］

考试 KET/PET/IELTS/TOEFL/PTE
科目 all

Put a word in each blank to complete the sentence.

每个空格填入一个单词，把句子补充完整。

blend

使混合，把……混成一体；使调和，融合

v. ［blend］

考试 TOEFL/IELTS/PTE
科目 listening

The old and new buildings blend together perfectly.

新旧建筑物相映成趣。

bless

赐福；祝福；使神圣

vt. ［bles］

考试 KET/PET/IELTS/TOEFL/PTE
科目 all

She blessed the newlyweds with a long and happy marriage.

她祝福新人拥有长长久久的幸福婚姻。

blind

失明的，瞎的；盲目的

adj. ［blaɪnd］

考试 KET/PET/IELTS/TOEFL/ PTE
科目 all

I started helping him run the business when he went blind.

他失明以后，我就开始帮他打理生意。

使失明；使眼花；使目眩

vt. ［blaɪnd］

考试 KET/PET/IELTS/TOEFL/ PTE
科目 all

The sun hit the windscreen, momentarily blinding him.
太阳照在挡风玻璃上，让他一时感觉目眩。

窗帘；百叶窗

n. ［blaɪnd］

考试 KET/PET/IELTS/TOEFL/ PTE
科目 all

Pulling the blinds up, she let some of the bright sunlight in.
她拉起窗帘，让一些明媚的阳光照了进来。

---

block

大块；街区；障碍物

n. ［blɒk］

考试 KET/PET/IELTS/TOEFL/ PTE
科目 all

His apartment is three blocks away from the police station.
他住在与警察局相隔三个街区的公寓里。

阻碍，妨碍；堵住（某人的路等）；拦截

vt. ［blɒk］

考试 KET/PET/IELTS/TOEFL/ PTE
科目 all

When the shrimp farm is built it will block the stream.
养虾场一旦建起来，将会截断这条河。

bloom

（常指供观赏的）花；兴旺时期

n. ［bluːm］

考试 KET/PET/IELTS/TOEFL/PTE
科目 all

The park is a picture when flowers are in bloom.
当鲜花盛开时，这个公园里的景色美极了。

开花；在青春时期

vi. ［bluːm］

考试 KET/PET/IELTS/TOEFL/PTE
科目 all

This plant blooms between May and June.
这种植物在 5 月至 6 月间开花。

blossom

（尤指果树或灌木的）花朵，花簇；花期；青春

n. ［ˈblɒsəm］

考试 TOEFL/IELTS/PTE
科目 listening

The cherry blossom came out early in Washington this year.
今年，华盛顿的樱花开得很早。

blow

吹，吹气；打气；吹奏；爆炸

v. ［bləʊ］

考试 KET/PET/IELTS/TOEFL/PTE
科目 all

A chill wind blew at the top of the hill.
山顶寒风呼啸。

挫折，打击；猛击；吹

n. ［bləʊ］

考试 KET/PET/IELTS/TOEFL/PTE
科目 all

Losing his job came as a terrible blow to him.
失业给他造成了沉重的打击。

board

木板；理事会，委员会，董事会

n. ［bɔːd］

考试 KET/PET/IELTS/TOEFL/
PTE
科目 all

Arthur wants to present his recommendation to the board at a meeting tomorrow.

亚瑟希望在明天的会议上把自己的建议提交给董事会。

上船（或火车、飞机、公共汽车等）

v. ［bɔːd］

考试 KET/PET/IELTS/TOEFL/
PTE
科目 all

I boarded the plane bound for England.

我登上了飞往英格兰的飞机。

boil

沸腾，煮沸；怒火中烧，异常气愤

v. ［bɔɪl］

考试 KET/PET/IELTS/TOEFL/
PTE
科目 all

I stood in the kitchen, waiting for the water to boil.

我站在厨房，等着水烧开。

boiling

炽热的，很热的

adj. ［ˈbɔɪlɪŋ］

考试 KET/PET/IELTS/TOEFL/
PTE
科目 all

Racial tension has reached a boiling point.

种族间的紧张状态已达到一触即发的程度。

bookshelf

书架

n. ［ˈbʊkʃelf］

考试 KET/PET/IELTS/TOEFL/
PTE
科目 all

Your bookshelf is overflowing with books you haven't read.

你的书架上堆满了你不曾读过的图书。

boost

使增长；使兴旺

vt. ［buːst］

考试 TOEFL/IELTS/PTE
科目 reading

The movie helped boost her screen career.
那部电影有助于她的银幕生涯的发展。

border

边，边界；花园中的花坛

n. ［ˈbɔːdə(r)］

考试 KET/PET/IELTS/TOEFL/
PTE
科目 all

The border between science fact and science fiction gets a bit fuzzy.
科学事实与科幻小说之间的界限变得有点儿模糊了。

和……毗邻，与……接壤；沿……的边

v. ［ˈbɔːdə(r)］

考试 KET/PET/IELTS/TOEFL/
PTE
科目 all

Meadows bordered the path to the woods.
通往树林的小路两边是草地。

bottom

底（部）；基础，根基；海底，湖底，水底

n. ［ˈbɒtəm］

考试 KET/PET/IELTS/TOEFL/
PTE
科目 all

The manufacturer's name is on the bottom of the plate.
制造厂商的名称在盘子背面。

boundary

边界，分界线

n. ［ˈbaʊndri］

考试 TOEFL/IELTS/PTE
科目 listening

Scientists continue to push back the boundaries of human knowledge.
科学家不断扩大人类知识的范围。

brain

（大）脑；（供食用的动物脑）髓；脑力，智力

n. ［breɪn］

考试 KET/PET/IELTS/TOEFL/ PTE
科目 all

Once you stop using your brain you soon go stale.

一旦停止用脑，你很快就会变得迟钝。

brave

勇敢的

adj. ［breɪv］

考试 KET/PET/IELTS/TOEFL/ PTE
科目 all

He was not brave enough to report the loss of the documents.

他没有勇气报告文件遗失。

勇敢地面对（危险等）

v. ［breɪv］

考试 KET/PET/IELTS/TOEFL/ PTE
科目 all

Thousands have braved icy rain to demonstrate their support.

数千人在寒冷的天气中冒雨赶来以示他们的支持。

Brazilian

巴西的

adj. ［brəˈzɪliən］

考试 KET/PET/IELTS/TOEFL/ PTE
科目 all

A senior Brazilian official has said his country favours an emerging-market candidate.

巴西的一位高级官员说，巴西支持一个新兴市场的候选人。

巴西人

n. ［brəˈzɪliən］

考试 KET/PET/IELTS/TOEFL/ PTE
科目 all

The sharp drop spurred the Brazilians into action.

这种急剧下跌促使巴西人采取了行动。

breathe

呼吸，呼出

v. ［briːð］

考试 KET/PET/IELTS/TOEFL/PTE
科目 all

Many people don't realize that they are breathing polluted air.

很多人没有意识到自己正在呼吸着受污染的空气。

breed

繁殖，生育；使养成；导致

v. ［briːd］

考试 TOEFL/IELTS
科目 writing

Frogs will usually breed in any convenient pond.

通常，青蛙会在任何条件适宜的池塘中繁殖。

bridge

桥；桥梁；纽带；鼻梁

n. ［brɪdʒ］

考试 KET/PET/IELTS/TOEFL/PTE
科目 all

Cultural exchanges are a way of building bridges between countries.

文化交流是各国之间建立联系的纽带。

在……上架桥

vt. ［brɪdʒ］

考试 KET/PET/IELTS/TOEFL/PTE
科目 all

A wooden plank bridged the stream.

一块木板横跨于溪流之上。

bright

明亮的，辉煌的；聪明的；欢快的，美好的

adj. ［braɪt］

考试 KET/PET/IELTS/TOEFL/PTE
科目 all

Her baby has bonny and bright blue eyes.

她的孩子有一双美丽而明亮的蓝眼睛。

broaden

变宽；(使) 扩大影响；增长

v. [ˈbrɔːdn]

考试 TOEFL/IELTS/PTE
科目 reading

Studying abroad can broaden the mind.
出国留学可以开阔视野。

brush

刷 (子)，毛刷；画笔

n. [brʌʃ]

考试 KET/PET/IELTS/TOEFL/
PTE
科目 all

I need a brush to clean my shoes.
我需要刷子来清洗我的鞋。

bubble

气泡，泡沫

n. [ˈbʌbl]

考试 KET/PET/IELTS/TOEFL/
PTE
科目 all

When the economic bubble burst, lots of people lost their jobs.
当经济泡沫破灭时，很多人失去了工作。

budget

预算

n. [ˈbʌdʒɪt]

考试 TOEFL/IELTS/PTE
科目 reading

We need to finish the task within the budget.
我们需要在预算内完成任务。

building

建筑 (物)，房屋，楼房

n. [ˈbɪldɪŋ]

考试 KET/PET/IELTS/TOEFL/
PTE
科目 all

The Leisure Center is a long and low modern building.
休闲中心是一座狭长而低矮的现代建筑。

bulk

大（量）；（大）体积；大块；巨大的体重（或重量、形状、身体等）

n. ［bʌlk］

考试 TOEFL/IELTS/PTE
科目 listening

Despite its bulk and weight, the car is extremely fast.
尽管这辆车体积大而且重，但是它的速度极快。

burden

担子，重担，负担

n. ［ˈbɜːdn］

考试 TOEFL/IELTS/PTE
科目 reading

The main burden of caring for old people falls on the state.
国家负担起了照顾老人的大部分责任。

burn

燃烧，烧着；烧毁；灼伤

v. ［bɜːn］

考试 KET/PET/IELTS/TOEFL/PTE
科目 all

There was a fire burning in the large fireplace.
大壁炉里火势正旺。

烧伤，灼伤

n. ［bɜːn］

考试 KET/PET/IELTS/TOEFL/PTE
科目 all

Pyrography is the art of creating an image in wood using burn marks.
烙画艺术是用烫痕在木头上创作形象。

burst

爆裂，胀开；突然出现；爆满，涨满

v. ［bɜːst］

考试 TOEFL/IELTS
科目 writing

The river burst its banks and flooded nearby towns.
那条河决堤淹没了附近的城镇。

bush

灌木（丛）

n. ［buʃ］

考试 KET/PET/IELTS/TOEFL/PTE

科目 all

Around the crevices of the rocks grew a few dwarf oaks and thick bushes of myrtles.

四周的岩石缝里生长着几株矮小的橡树和茂密的香桃木花丛。

business

商业，生意；商务，业务；职责；事件；企业，公司

n. ［ˈbɪznəs］

考试 KET/PET/IELTS/TOEFL/PTE

科目 all

The new regulations will put many small businesses out of business.

新法规将使很多小企业关闭。

butter

黄油，奶油

n. ［ˈbʌtə(r)］

考试 KET/PET/IELTS/TOEFL/PTE

科目 all

The vegetable was dressed sparingly with butter, salt, and pepper.

蔬菜里面黄油、盐和胡椒加得很少。

涂黄油于……上

v. ［ˈbʌtə(r)］

考试 KET/PET/IELTS/TOEFL/PTE

科目 all

She buttered three thick slices of bread.

她在三片厚面包上涂了黄油。

butterfly

蝴蝶

n. ［ˈbʌtəflaɪ］

考试 KET/PET/IELTS/TOEFL/PTE

科目 all

A butterfly is produced by metamorphosis from a caterpillar.

蝴蝶是由毛虫蜕变而成的。

button

纽扣；按钮（开关）

n. ［'bʌtn］

考试 KET/PET/IELTS/TOEFL/PTE
科目 all

Choose "printer" from the menu and click with the right mouse button.

从菜单中选择"打印机"，然后点击鼠标右键。

扣紧；扣上纽扣

v. ［'bʌtn］

考试 KET/PET/IELTS/TOEFL/PTE
科目 all

He hurriedly buttoned（up）his jacket.

他急忙扣上了夹克衫的扣子。

bypass

旁道，旁路；搭桥术

n. ［'baɪpɑːs］

考试 TOEFL/IELTS/PTE
科目 listening

Dean was elated that his second heart bypass had been successful.

迪安的第二次心脏搭桥手术成功了，他很开心。

C

calculate

计算，核算；预测，推测

vt. [ˈkælkjuleɪt]

考试 KET/PET/IELTS/TOEFL/PTE
科目 all

You will need to calculate how much time the assignment will take.

你需要算一算多长时间才能完成分配的任务。

calculation

计算，计算结果；估计，预测，推测

n. [ˌkælkjuˈleɪʃn]

考试 KET/PET/IELTS/TOEFL/PTE
科目 all

The authors call their calculations demographic, not political.

作者称其计算具有人口统计学性质，而不带政治含义。

calendar

日历；历法；日程表

n. [ˈkælɪndə(r)]

考试 KET/PET/IELTS/TOEFL/PTE
科目 all

The 15th of the first month in the lunar calendar is the Lantern Festival.

阴历正月十五是元宵节。

calm

镇静的；（海洋）风平浪静的；（天气）无风的

adj. [kɑːm]

考试 KET/PET/IELTS/TOEFL/PTE
科目 all

Please remain calm, sir. Just give me your name and your location.

请保持镇静，先生。告诉我你的名字和所在地点。

平静

n. ［kɑːm］

考试 KET/PET/IELTS/TOEFL/
PTE
科目 all

It's the calm that precedes a storm.
这是暴风雨到来前的平静。

（使）平静，（使）镇静

v. ［kɑːm］

考试 KET/PET/IELTS/TOEFL/
PTE
科目 all

Calm the mind and promote mentality.
宁神益志。

camel

骆驼

n. ［ˈkæml］

考试 KET/PET/IELTS/TOEFL/
PTE
科目 all

The last straw breaks the camel's back.
最后一根草，压断骆驼背。

camera

照相机，摄影机

n. ［ˈkæmərə］

考试 KET/PET/IELTS/TOEFL/
PTE
科目 all

The case involved official secrets, so it was held in camera.
该案件涉及官方机密，所以进行秘密审讯。

camp

野营，营地；帐篷；阵营

n. ［kæmp］

考试 KET/PET/IELTS/TOEFL/
PTE
科目 all

The commanding officer made a circuit of the camp.
指挥官在营地巡视了一周。

露营，宿营；借住，借宿

vi. ［kæmp］

考试 KET/PET/IELTS/TOEFL/
PTE
科目 all

They camped out a night in order to relax themselves.

他们为了好好放松一下决定在外面住宿一晚上。

camping

野营度假

n. ［'kæmpɪŋ］

考试 KET/PET/IELTS/TOEFL/
PTE
科目 all

Yellowstone has numerous recreational opportunities, including hiking, camping, boating, fishing and sightseeing.

黄石公园有许多娱乐机会，包括徒步旅行、露营、划船、钓鱼以及观光。

cancel

删去；取消

v. ［'kænsl］

考试 KET/PET/IELTS/TOEFL/
PTE
科目 all

The advantages and disadvantages would appear to cancel each other out.

看来是利弊参半。

canvass

游说，拉选票

v. ［'kænvəs］

考试 TOEFL/IELTS
科目 writing

Party workers are busy canvassing local residents.

党务工作者正忙于游说当地居民。

capability

能力，才能；性能

n. ［ˌkeɪpə'bɪləti］

考试 TOEFL/IELTS/PTE
科目 reading

Studies have shown that unlimited options paralyze our decision making capability.

研究表明，无穷无尽的选择让我们失去了做决定的能力。

capable

有本领的，有能力的

adj. [ˈkeɪpəbl]

考试 TOEFL/IELTS/PTE
科目 reading

Capable workers are the lifeblood of the business.
能干的工人是企业的生命力。

capitalize

用大写字母书写；资本化；变卖资产，变现

v. [ˈkæpɪtəlaɪz]

考试 TOEFL/IELTS/PTE
科目 reading

The team failed to capitalize on their early lead.
这个队未能充分利用开场时领先的优势。

captain

首领，队长；船长；上尉

n. [ˈkæptɪn]

考试 KET/PET/IELTS/TOEFL/
PTE
科目 all

She was captain of the hockey team at school.
她过去是学校曲棍球队的队长。

capture

捕获，俘虏；夺得，攻占

v. [ˈkæptʃə(r)]

考试 TOEFL/IELTS/PTE
科目 listening

The company has now captured almost 90% of the market.
这家公司现已占有几乎90%的市场份额。

careful

小心的，仔细的；细致的，精心的，慎重的

adj. [ˈkeəfl]

考试 KET/PET/IELTS/TOEFL/
PTE
科目 all

After careful consideration the HR manager decided to offer the young girl a job.
经过慎重考虑后，人事经理决定给那个年轻的女孩提供一个工作机会。

careless

粗心的，漫不经心的

adj. [ˈkeələs]

考试 KET/PET/IELTS/TOEFL/
PTE
科目 all

Many accidents happen because people are careless.

很多事故是由人们的粗心引起的。

carpet

地毯

n. [ˈkɑːpɪt]

考试 KET/PET/IELTS/TOEFL/
PTE
科目 all

The red carpet has been rolled ready for the royal party and special guests.

为皇室成员和贵宾们准备的红地毯已被铺好。

cart

马车；手推车

n. [kɑːt]

考试 KET/PET/IELTS/TOEFL/
PTE
科目 all

The farmer harnessed the horse to the cart.

农夫把马套到了马车上。

用车装载

vt. [kɑːt]

考试 KET/PET/IELTS/TOEFL/
PTE
科目 all

The rubbish is then carted away for recycling.

垃圾随后被运去进行回收处理。

carton

纸盒；纸板箱；塑料箱

n. [ˈkɑːtn]

考试 TOEFL/IELTS/PTE
科目 listening

They carefully packed the fragile china into cartons.

他们小心地将易碎瓷器装入了纸箱。

cartoon

漫画；动画片

n. [kɑːˈtuːn]

考试 KET/PET/IELTS/TOEFL/PTE
科目 all

A newspaper cartoon is an amusing drawing, usually about some event in the news.
报纸上的漫画是一种风趣的图画，通常是针对某一时事的。

carve

雕刻；切（熟肉等）

v. [kɑːv]

考试 TOEFL/IELTS
科目 writing

The statue was carved out of a single piece of stone.
这座雕像是用整块石料雕成的。

case

箱，盒，容器；情况，事实；病例；案件；病人，伤员

n. [keɪs]

考试 KET/PET/IELTS/TOEFL/PTE
科目 all

The most serious cases were treated at the scene of the accident.
受伤最严重的人在事故现场得到了救治。

cashier

出纳员

n. [kæˈʃɪə(r)]

考试 KET/PET/IELTS/TOEFL/PTE
科目 all

The cheques must be signed in front of the cashier at the bank.
必须当着银行出纳员的面在这些支票上签名。

cast

投，掷，抛；投射；铸造；分配角色

v. [kɑːst]

考试 TOEFL/IELTS
科目 writing

The sad news cast a shadow over the proceedings.
这个坏消息给事件的进程蒙上了一层阴影。

catastrophe

灾难，灾祸；不幸事件，困难

n. [kə'tæstrəfi]

考试 TOEFL/IELTS/PTE
科目 reading

Early warning of rising water levels prevented a major catastrophe.

提前发出的上涨水位警报防止了一次重大灾害。

cause

原因；动机；事业；目标

n. [kɔːz]

考试 KET/PET/IELTS/TOEFL/PTE
科目 all

Drinking and driving is one of the most common causes of traffic accidents.

酒后驾车是导致交通事故的最常见原因之一。

使产生，引起

vt. [kɔːz]

考试 KET/PET/IELTS/TOEFL/PTE
科目 all

The poor harvest caused prices to rise sharply.

歉收导致价格急剧上涨。

caution

小心；告诫；警告

n. ['kɔːʃn]

考试 KET/PET/IELTS/TOEFL/PTE
科目 all

Some cautions must be mentioned—for example, good tools are essential to do the job well.

有些警句必须提及，如：工欲善其事，必先利其器。

告诫，提醒；警告

v. ['kɔːʃn]

考试 KET/PET/IELTS/TOEFL/PTE
科目 all

Suspects must be cautioned before any questions are asked.

嫌疑犯在回答问题前必须得到提醒。

cautious

小心的，谨慎的

adj. [ˈkɔːʃəs]

考试 TOEFL/IELTS/PTE
科目 listening

They expressed cautious optimism about a solution to the crisis.
他们对解决危机持谨慎乐观的态度。

cease

停止，结束

v. [siːs]

考试 TOEFL/IELTS
科目 writing

Welfare payments cease as soon as an individual starts a job.
一旦就业，即停发福利救济。

celebrate

庆祝，庆贺；颂扬，赞美

v. [ˈselɪbreɪt]

考试 KET/PET/IELTS/TOEFL/PTE
科目 all

The streets are flagged to celebrate the victory.
街道上悬挂旗帜以庆祝胜利。
Alex received the offer of his first job and went out to celebrate.
亚历克斯收到了第一份工作录用通知，出去庆祝了。

celebration

庆祝仪式，庆典；颂扬

n. [ˌselɪˈbreɪʃn]

考试 KET/PET/IELTS/TOEFL/PTE
科目 all

People gathered in the hall for the celebration on the eve of the National Day.
国庆节前夕，人们聚集在礼堂开庆祝会。

cell

细胞；小房间；蜂房；电池

n. [sel]

考试 KET/PET/IELTS/TOEFL/PTE
科目 all

Adult stem cells are thought by scientists to be less versatile than their embryonic equivalents.

在科学家看来，成年人干细胞没有胚胎干细胞那样神通广大。

cement

水泥，结合剂

n. [sɪˈment]

考试 TOEFL/IELTS/PTE
科目 listening

Steel，cement and labour have all got cheaper.

钢铁、水泥以及劳动力的费用都有所下降。

censorship

审查，检查；审查制度

n. [ˈsensəʃɪp]

考试 TOEFL/IELTS/PTE
科目 reading

The decree imposed strict censorship of the media.

这项法令强制实行严格的媒体审查制度。

cent

（货币单位）分，分币

n. [sent]

考试 KET/PET/IELTS/TOEFL/PTE
科目 all

The admission fee is 20 cents each.

每张门票 20 美分。

central

中心的，中央的，中枢的；主要的

adj. [ˈsentrəl]

考试 KET/PET/IELTS/TOEFL/PTE
科目 all

The car has power steering and a central locking system.

这辆汽车装有动力转向和中枢锁闭系统。

C

center

中心，中央，中间

n. [ˈsentə(r)]

考试 KET/PET/IELTS/TOEFL/PTE
科目 all

Small towns in South India serve as economic and cultural centers for surrounding villagers.
印度南部的小城镇是周围村庄的经济和文化中心。

集中；以……为中心

v. [ˈsentə(r)]

考试 KET/PET/IELTS/TOEFL/PTE
科目 all

Most of the fighting was centered in the north of the capital.
多数打斗集中在首都的北部地区。
State occasions always centered around the king himself.
国事活动总是以国王为中心。

cereal

谷物，谷类食物；麦片

n. [ˈsɪəriəl]

考试 KET/PET/IELTS/TOEFL/PTE
科目 all

Cereal makers claim that children who eat cereal consume more nutrients.
麦片生产商们认为儿童吃麦片可以摄入更多的营养物质。

ceremony

典礼，仪式；礼节

n. [ˈserəməni]

考试 KET/PET/IELTS/TOEFL/PTE
科目 all

The ceremony proceeded in a solemn atmosphere.
仪式在庄严的气氛中进行着。

certain

某，某一；某些；一定的，确信的，可靠的

adj. [ˈsəːtn]

考试 KET/PET/IELTS/TOEFL/PTE
科目 all

Certain people present were unwilling to discuss the matter further.

某些在场的人不愿意进一步讨论这个问题。

certainly

一定，必定，无疑；当然

adv. [ˈsəːtnli]

考试 KET/PET/IELTS/TOEFL/PTE
科目 all

Certainly, the early learning years are crucial to a child's educational development.

毫无疑问，最初几年的启蒙教育对儿童的发展至关重要。

certify

（尤指书面）证明；证实

vt. [ˈsəːtɪfaɪ]

考试 TOEFL/IELTS
科目 writing

The accounts were certified correct by the finance department.

账目经财务部门证实无误。

chairman

主席，议长，会长，董事长

n. [ˈtʃeəmən]

考试 KET/PET/IELTS/TOEFL/PTE
科目 all

The chairman of the company presented the annual report.

公司董事长提交了年度报告。

challenge

挑战；提出异议

n. [ˈtʃælɪndʒ]

考试 KET/PET/IELTS/TOEFL/PTE
科目 all

Destruction of the environment is one of the most serious challenges we face.

环境的破坏是我们所面临的最严峻挑战之一。

对……怀疑；拒绝接受；向……挑战

vt. [ˈtʃælɪndʒ]

考试 KET/PET/IELTS/TOEFL/PTE
科目 all

This discovery challenges traditional beliefs.

这项发现是对传统观念的冲击。

challenging

具有挑战性的

adj. [ˈtʃælɪndʒɪŋ]

考试 KET/PET/IELTS/TOEFL/PTE
科目 all

Thesis writing is a challenging writing task.

论文写作是一项具有挑战性的任务。

champion

冠军；拥护

n. [ˈtʃæmpiən]

考试 KET/PET/IELTS/TOEFL/PTE
科目 all

This country is an export champion largely because it has done many things right.

这个国家是出口国冠军，主要是因为它在许多方面做对了。

为……而斗争，支持，拥护；捍卫

vt. [ˈtʃæmpiən]

考试 KET/PET/IELTS/TOEFL/PTE
科目 all

He has always championed the cause of labourers' rights.

他一直在为争取劳动者的权利而斗争。

channel

海峡；水道；频道，波段；渠道，途径；方式，手段

n. [ˈtʃænl]

考试 KET/PET/IELTS/TOEFL/PTE
科目 all

The email is a useful channel of communication between teachers and students.

电子邮件是师生之间沟通的有效渠道。

chaos

混乱，杂乱

n. [ˈkeɪɒs]

考试 TOEFL/IELTS/PTE
科目 listening

It's an impossible job, but the alternative is chaos.
这是一项艰巨的工作，但是舍此就是混沌。

chapter

章；回，篇

n. [ˈtʃæptə(r)]

考试 KET/PET/IELTS/TOEFL/PTE
科目 all

Current problems mark only the latest chapter in a long story.
如今的难题只是一个漫长故事中的最新篇章。

character

性格，品质，特性；特点，特色；人物，角色；字母，符号

n. [ˈkærəktə(r)]

考试 KET/PET/IELTS/TOEFL/PTE
科目 all

The character of the neighbourhood hasn't changed at all.
这片住宅区的风貌依旧。

characteristic

特有的；典型的；独特的

adj. [ˌkærəktəˈrɪstɪk]

考试 TOEFL/IELTS/PTE
科目 listening

She spoke with characteristic enthusiasm.
她说话时带着特有的热情。

charge

要价；控告，指控；冲锋；充电

v. [tʃɑːdʒ]

考试 KET/PET/IELTS/TOEFL/PTE
科目 all

The shaver can be charged up and used when travelling.
这种剃须刀可以充电供旅行中使用。

C

charity

赈济；慈善机构；仁爱

n. [ˈtʃærəti]

考试 KET/PET/IELTS/TOEFL/PTE
科目 all

Most of the runners in the London Marathon are raising money for charity.

大多数选手参加伦敦马拉松比赛是为慈善事业募集资金。

chart

图表；海图

n. [tʃɑːt]

考试 KET/PET/IELTS/TOEFL/PTE
科目 all

Such a diagram is called a flow chart and the path of action is easily seen in the chart.

这样的图表叫作流程图，从图中很容易看出动作的过程。

chase

追逐，追赶；努力获得，争取得到；雕刻，镂刻

v. [tʃeɪs]

考试 TOEFL/IELTS
科目 writing

Too many people are chasing too few jobs nowadays.

如今，太多的人在角逐寥寥无几的工作职位。

chat

闲谈，聊天

v. [tʃæt]

考试 KET/PET/IELTS/TOEFL/PTE
科目 all

The friends met occasionally to chat about the good old days at school.

朋友们偶尔相聚，畅谈上学时的美好时光。

闲谈，聊天

n. [tʃæt]

考试 KET/PET/IELTS/TOEFL/PTE
科目 all

The interview resolved itself into a pleasant chat.

会谈变成了愉快的闲聊。

cheat

欺骗；作弊

v. [tʃiːt]

考试 KET/PET/IELTS/TOEFL/PTE
科目 all

Many people feel cheated by the government's refusal to hold a referendum.
由于政府拒绝举行公民投票表决，许多人觉得上当受骗了。
The student received a severe reprimand for cheating in the terminal examination.
这名学生因在期末考试中作弊而受到了一次严重警告处分。

骗子；欺诈，欺骗行为

n. [tʃiːt]

考试 KET/PET/IELTS/TOEFL/PTE
科目 all

He was publicly exposed as a liar and a cheat.
他说谎者和骗子的面目被公之于众。

check

检查，查看；调查，审查；控制；约束

n. [tʃek]

考试 KET/PET/IELTS/TOEFL/PTE
科目 all

A cold spring will provide a natural check on the number of insects.
寒冷的春季会自然控制昆虫的数量。

检查；核实；制止

v. [tʃek]

考试 KET/PET/IELTS/TOEFL/PTE
科目 all

Check the electricity and water before setting off.
出发前检查一下水电。

checkout

结账，结账离店时间

n. ['tʃekaʊt]

考试 KET/PET/IELTS/TOEFL/PTE
科目 all

At checkout, your bill will be printed for you.

结账时，旅馆会把你的账单打印给你。

check-up

检查；（尤指）体检

n. ['tʃek‚ʌp]

考试 KET/PET/IELTS/TOEFL/PTE
科目 all

We should do regular check-ups to prevent diseases.

我们应该定期做检查以预防疾病。

cheer

欢呼声，喝彩声

n. [tʃɪə(r)]

考试 KET/PET/IELTS/TOEFL/PTE
科目 all

A great cheer went up from the crowd.

人群中爆发出一阵热烈的欢呼声。

振奋，高兴，欢呼

v. [tʃɪə(r)]

考试 KET/PET/IELTS/TOEFL/PTE
科目 all

The crowd cheered the President as he drove slowly by.

当总统的车缓缓驶过时，人群向他欢呼致意。

chemistry

化学

n. ['kemɪstri]

考试 KET/PET/IELTS/TOEFL/PTE
科目 all

Alchemy paved the way for the modern science of chemistry.

炼金术为现代化学科学铺了路。

cheque

支票

n. [tʃek]

考试 KET/PET/IELTS/TOEFL/PTE
科目 all

The bank adds on a 5% handling charge for changing traveller's cheque.

兑换旅行支票时，银行要收取5%的手续费。

cherish

珍爱，钟爱；爱护；抱有（希望）；怀有（情感）

vt. ['tʃerɪʃ]

考试 TOEFL/IELTS/PTE
科目 reading

Most Americans cherish freedom and independence.

大多数美国人都钟爱自由和独立。

chess

国际象棋

n. [tʃes]

考试 KET/PET/IELTS/TOEFL/PTE
科目 all

Chess is a highly intellectual game.

国际象棋是需要高智商的比赛项目。

chest

胸腔，胸膛；箱，柜

n. [tʃest]

考试 KET/PET/IELTS/TOEFL/PTE
科目 all

The chest contained the personal belongings of a seaman.

箱子里装有一个海员的私人物品。

childhood

幼年，童年，孩童时期

n. ['tʃaɪldhʊd]

考试 KET/PET/IELTS/TOEFL/PTE
科目 all

Her interest in flowers steps from her childhood in the countryside.

她对花卉的兴趣始于她在乡下度过的孩童时期。

chill

寒冷；寒意；凉意

n. ［tʃɪl］

考试 KET/PET/IELTS/TOEFL/
PTE
科目 all

A small fire was burning to take the chill of the room.

房间里生着小火炉驱寒。

寒冷；冷飕飕的

adj. ［tʃɪl］

考试 KET/PET/IELTS/TOEFL/
PTE
科目 all

He turned up his coat collar against the chill wind.

他竖起外套的衣领以抵御寒风。

（使）冰冷；（使）冷却；冷藏

v. ［tʃɪl］

考试 KET/PET/IELTS/TOEFL/
PTE
科目 all

Let the pudding chill for an hour until set.

把布丁冷却一小时直至凝固成形。

church

教堂；教会，教派；礼拜仪式

n. ［tʃɜːtʃ］

考试 KET/PET/IELTS/TOEFL/
PTE
科目 all

The Church has a duty to condemn violence.

基督教会有义务谴责暴力。

cigarette

香烟，纸烟，卷烟

n. ［ˌsɪgəˈret］

考试 KET/PET/IELTS/TOEFL/
PTE
科目 all

The China National Tobacco Corporation is the world's largest cigarette maker.

中国烟草总公司是全球最大的卷烟生产商。

circle

圆，圆圈；圆周；圈子，阶层；周期，循环

n. [ˈsɜːkl]

考试 KET/PET/IELTS/TOEFL/ PTE
科目 all

She walked the horse round in a circle.
她牵着马兜圈子。

盘旋；环绕，旋转

v. [ˈsɜːkl]

考试 KET/PET/IELTS/TOEFL/ PTE
科目 all

The plane circled the airport to burn up excess fuel.
飞机在机场上空盘旋以消耗多余的燃料。

circulate

（使）循环；（使）流通；（使）流传，传播

v. [ˈsɜːkjəleɪt]

考试 TOEFL/IELTS
科目 writing

This disease prevents the blood from circulating freely.
这种疾病阻碍了血液的顺畅循环。

circulation

循环；（货币等）流通

n. [ˌsɜːkjəˈleɪʃn]

考试 TOEFL/IELTS/PTE
科目 listening

A number of forged tickets are in circulation.
有一些伪造的入场券在流通。

cite

引用；举例，传讯

vt. [saɪt]

考试 TOEFL/IELTS/PTE
科目 listening

She cited a passage from the President's speech.
她引用了一段总统的演讲。

citizen

公民；市民，居民

n. [ˈsɪtɪzn]

考试 KET/PET/IELTS/TOEFL/PTE
科目 all

Under the new system, the ordinary citizen has more clout.

在新体制下，一般市民拥有了更大的影响力。

civilize

使文明，开化

v. [ˈsɪvəlaɪz]

考试 TOEFL/IELTS
科目 writing

School education helps civilize the people which is one of the civil rights.

学校教育作为一项公民权，使人们文明起来。

clarify

澄清，使液体清洁

v. [ˈklærəfaɪ]

考试 TOEFL/IELTS/PTE
科目 listening

In an attempt to clarify the contradiction, the researchers repeated the study.

为了弄清为什么会出现这种矛盾，研究者们再次进行了这项研究。

classic

第一流的，最优秀的；传统的；典型的

adj. [ˈklæsɪk]

考试 KET/PET/IELTS/TOEFL/PTE
科目 all

The car neatly blends classic styling into a smooth modern package.

这款汽车巧妙地将经典式样融入了流线型现代设计中。

优秀的典范；经典作品，名著

n. [ˈklæsɪk]

考试 KET/PET/IELTS/TOEFL/PTE
科目 all

War and Peace is a literary classic.

《战争与和平》是一部经典文学著作。

classical

经典的；古典的；传统的

adj. ['klæsɪkl]

考试 KET/PET/IELTS/TOEFL/PTE
科目 all

The classical Chinese poetry paid much attention to implication.

中国古诗非常注重言外之意。

classify

把……分类，分等级

vt. ['klæsɪfaɪ]

考试 TOEFL/IELTS/PTE
科目 listening

The books in the library are classified according to subjects.

图书馆里的书按学科分类。

clerk

职员，办事员；店员

n. [klɑːk]

考试 KET/PET/IELTS/TOEFL/PTE
科目 all

The clerk was elevated to a managerial position.

那名职员被提拔起来当经理。

cleverness

聪明，机灵

n. ['klevənəs]

考试 KET/PET/IELTS/TOEFL/PTE
科目 all

Her cleverness and talent helped her look more beautiful than ever.

她的聪明才智使她更显得美貌非凡。

client

客户，委托人

n. ['klaɪənt]

考试 TOEFL/IELTS/PTE
科目 reading

Social workers must consider the best interest of their clients in every situation.

社会工作者必须考虑其委托人在各种情况下的最佳利益。

climate

气候；风气，社会思潮

n. [ˈklaɪmət]

考试 KET/PET/IELTS/TOEFL/PTE
科目 all

We need to create a climate in which business can prosper.
我们需要创造有利于生意兴隆的环境氛围。

clinic

诊所；门诊部

n. [ˈklɪnɪk]

考试 KET/PET/IELTS/TOEFL/PTE
科目 all

The letter suggested that a new clinic should be built.
来信提议修建一个新诊疗所。

closely

紧密地；接近地

adv. [ˈkləʊsli]

考试 KET/PET/IELTS/TOEFL/PTE
科目 all

Taking exercise is closely related to health.
运动与健康息息相关。

cloth

（一块）布；织物，衣料

n. [klɒθ]

考试 KET/PET/IELTS/TOEFL/PTE
科目 all

Wipe the table surface with a damp cloth.
用湿布擦拭桌面。

clothe

（给……）穿衣；提供……衣服

vt. [kləʊð]

考试 KET/PET/IELTS/TOEFL/PTE
科目 all

Climbing plants clothed the courtyard walls.
攀缘植物给院墙披上了绿装。

cloudy

多云的，阴（天）的；混浊的，模糊的

adj. [ˈklaʊdi]

考试 KET/PET/IELTS/TOEFL/ PTE
科目 all

Cloudy days are better for photos than bright sunny days because the clouds diffuse the sun's light.
多云的天气会比万里无云的晴朗天气更适合拍照，因为云彩可以使太阳光线变得很柔和。

coach

长途汽车，长途客车；教师；教练

n. [kəʊtʃ]

考试 KET/PET/IELTS/TOEFL/ PTE
科目 all

The rookie complained that the coach kept him mostly on the bench.
新来的运动员抱怨教练老让他做替补。

辅导；训练

vt. [kəʊtʃ]

考试 KET/PET/IELTS/TOEFL/ PTE
科目 all

She has coached many young singers.
她培养了许多青年歌手。

coal

煤，煤块

n. [kəʊl]

考试 KET/PET/IELTS/TOEFL/ PTE
科目 all

Coal is an essentially nonrenewable resource.
煤是不可再生资源。

coast

海岸，海滨

n. [kəʊst]

考试 KET/PET/IELTS/TOEFL/ PTE
科目 all

Camp sites are usually situated along the coast, close to beaches.
野营地一般都位于海滨，靠近沙滩。

code

规则；代号；密码

n. ［kəʊd］

考试 KET/PET/IELTS/TOEFL/PTE
科目 all

In the event of the machine not operating correctly, an error code will appear.

如果机器运转不正常，就会出现错误代码。

把……译成密码；为……编码

vt. ［kəʊd］

考试 KET/PET/IELTS/TOEFL/PTE
科目 all

Product orders should be coded according to where they will be shipped.

产品订单应按产品发往地点编码。

coherent

一致的，协调的；（话语等）条理清楚的，合乎逻辑的

adj. ［kəʊˈhɪərənt］

考试 TOEFL/IELTS/PTE
科目 listening

He has failed to work out a coherent strategy for modernizing the service.

他未能制订出连贯的策略来实现服务的现代化。

collapse

倒塌，坍塌；（精神）垮下来

v. ［kəˈlæps］

考试 TOEFL/IELTS
科目 writing

The roof collapsed under the weight of snow.

房顶在积雪的重压下突然坍塌下来。

collect

收集，搜集；领取，接走；收（税等）；聚集，堆积

v. ［kəˈlekt］

考试 KET/PET/IELTS/TOEFL/PTE
科目 all

That piano has been sitting collecting dust for years now.

那架钢琴至今已尘封多年。

collection

收藏（品），收集（物）

n. [kəˈlekʃn]

考试 KET/PET/IELTS/TOEFL/PTE
科目 all

The precious painting comes from a soldier's private collection.

这幅珍贵的画来自一名军人的私人收藏。

college

学院；高等专科学校；大学

n. [ˈkɒlɪdʒ]

考试 KET/PET/IELTS/TOEFL/PTE
科目 all

This university is composed of five colleges and one graduate school.

这所大学由五个学院和一个研究生院组成。

collide

碰撞，相撞；冲突，抵触

vi. [kəˈlaɪd]

考试 TOEFL/IELTS/PTE
科目 listening

The car and the van collided head-on in thick fog.

那辆小轿车和一辆货车在浓雾中迎面相撞。

colourful

颜色鲜艳的，色彩丰富的

adj. [ˈkʌləfl]

考试 TOEFL/IELTS/PTE
科目 listening

The male birds are more colourful than the females.

这种鸟雄性比雌性更加色彩艳丽。

colourless

无色的；苍白的；无趣的，枯燥的

adj. [ˈkʌlələs]

考试 KET/PET/IELTS/TOEFL/PTE
科目 all

Aniline is an oily but colourless and water soluble chemical intermediate that is a probable carcinogen.

苯胺是一种油性、无色、可溶于水的化学中间体，属可能致癌物。

column

柱，圆柱状物；书报上的栏；纵列

n. ［ˈkɒləm］

考试 KET/PET/IELTS/TOEFL/PTE
科目 all

The well-known singer's divorce filled a lot of column inches in the national papers.
这位著名歌手的离婚引起了多家全国性报纸的关注。

combat

战斗，搏斗

n. ［ˈkɒmbæt］

考试 TOEFL/IELTS/PTE
科目 listening

The soldiers were engaged in hand-to-hand combat with the enemy.
士兵们与敌人展开了肉搏。

combine

联合；（使）结合

v. ［kəmˈbaɪn］

考试 TOEFL/IELTS
科目 writing

We should try to combine exercise with a healthy diet.
我们应该尽力把锻炼和健康饮食结合起来。

comedian

喜剧演员

n. ［kəˈmiːdiən］

考试 KET/PET/IELTS/TOEFL/PTE
科目 all

Unlike clowns, comedians' clothes are usually not very strange.
与丑角不同，喜剧演员的服装通常并不奇怪。

comedy

喜剧；喜剧性事件；滑稽；幽默

n. ［ˈkɒmədi］

考试 KET/PET/IELTS/TOEFL/PTE
科目 all

He didn't appreciate the comedy of the situation.
他未领略到这种局面的滑稽可笑之处。

comfort

舒适，安逸；安慰，慰问

n. [ˈkʌmfət]

考试 KET/PET/IELTS/TOEFL/
PTE
科目 all

The basketball shoes are designed for comfort and performance.

这些篮球鞋设计得穿起来舒服，利于发挥成绩。

安慰，使舒适

vt. [ˈkʌmfət]

考试 KET/PET/IELTS/TOEFL/
PTE
科目 all

She comforted herself with the thought that it would soon be spring.

她想着春天很快就要来临，以此来宽慰自己。

comfortable

舒适的，舒服的；感到舒适的，安逸的；愉快放松的，自在的

adj. [ˈkʌmfətəbl]

考试 KET/PET/IELTS/TOEFL/
PTE
科目 all

Please make yourself comfortable while I get some coffee.

我去冲咖啡，您别拘束。

comic

滑稽的；喜剧的

adj. [ˈkɒmɪk]

考试 KET/PET/IELTS/TOEFL/
PTE
科目 all

She can always be relied on to provide comic relief at a boring party.

在沉闷的聚会上，她总能让人喜笑颜开。

连环画杂志；喜剧演员

n. [ˈkɒmɪk]

考试 KET/PET/IELTS/TOEFL/
PTE
科目 all

The comic skit sents up the foolishness of young men in love.

那幅漫画勾勒出了热恋中男子的痴态。

commence

开始

v. ［kəˈmens］

考试 TOEFL/IELTS
科目 writing

The day commenced with a welcome from the principal.

那天由校长致欢迎辞开始。

commend

称赞；推荐；委托保管

vt. ［kəˈmend］

考试 TOEFL/IELTS/PTE
科目 listening

She is an excellent worker and I commend her to you without reservation.

她工作出色，我毫无保留地把她推荐给你。

comment

评论；批评；解释

n. ［ˈkɒment］

考试 KET/PET/IELTS/TOEFL/
PTE
科目 all

The results are a clear comment on government education policy.

这些结果是对政府教育政策明显的批评。

表达意见

v. ［ˈkɒment］

考试 KET/PET/IELTS/TOEFL/
PTE
科目 all

A spokesperson commented that levels of carbon dioxide were very high.

发言人称二氧化碳的含量很高。

commitment

承诺；许诺；献身；奉献

n. ［kəˈmitmənt］

考试 TOEFL/IELTS/PTE
科目 reading

The company's commitment to providing quality at a reasonable price has been vital to its success.

这家公司致力于提供质优价廉的产品，这对它的成功起了决定性的作用。

communicate

传达，传送；交流；沟通

v. [kə'mjuːnɪkeɪt]

考试 KET/PET/IELTS/TOEFL/
PTE
科目 all

Dolphins use sound to communicate with each other.

海豚用声音相互沟通。

communication

通信；交往；交流；表达；交通联系

n. [kəˌmjuːnɪ'keɪʃn]

考试 KET/PET/IELTS/TOEFL/
PTE
科目 all

Snow has prevented communication with the outside world for three days.

大雪使得与外界的沟通联系中断了三天。

community

同一地区的全体居民；社会，社区；团体

n. [kə'mjuːnəti]

考试 KET/PET/IELTS/TOEFL/
PTE
科目 all

The local community was shocked by the murders.

当地社会对这些谋杀案感到震惊。

compact

紧密的；紧凑的

adj. [kəm'pækt]

考试 TOEFL/IELTS/PTE
科目 listening

The kitchen was compact but well equipped.

这间厨房虽然空间小，但设备齐全。

company

公司；陪伴；宾客；连（队）；（一）群，队，伙

n. ['kʌmpəni]

考试 KET/PET/IELTS/TOEFL/
PTE
科目 all

It is bad manners to whisper in company.

在众人面前窃窃私语是不礼貌的行为。

comparative

比较的，相比的；相对的

adj. [kəmˈpærətɪv]

考试 TOEFL/IELTS/PTE
科目 listening

The company is a comparative newcomer to the software market.
就软件市场来说，这家公司相对而言就是新手了。

compare

比较，对照；将……比作

v. [kəmˈpeə(r)]

考试 KET/PET/IELTS/TOEFL/PTE
科目 all

Standards in health care have improved enormously compared to those of 60 years ago.
与 60 年前相比，卫生保健水平得到了极大的提高。

compatible

可共存的；兼容的

adj. [kəmˈpætəbl]

考试 TOEFL/IELTS/PTE
科目 listening

The donor's blood is compatible with the recipient's.
供血者的血和受血者的血是相容的。

compel

强迫，迫使

vt. [kəmˈpel]

考试 TOEFL/IELTS/PTE
科目 reading

The law can compel fathers to make regular payments for their children.
这项法律可强制父亲定期支付子女的费用。

compensate

赔偿，补偿

v. [ˈkɒmpenseɪt]

考试 TOEFL/IELTS
科目 writing

To ease financial difficulties, farmers could be compensated for their loss of subsidies.
为了缓解经济困难，农场主们损失的补贴会得到补偿。

compete

参加比赛；竞争；对抗

vi. [kəmˈpiːt]

考试 KET/PET/IELTS/TOEFL/
PTE
科目 all

Small traders cannot compete in the face of cheap foreign imports.

面对廉价的外国进口商品，经营规模很小的商人无法与之抗衡。

competition

比赛，比赛会；竞争

n. [ˌkɒmpəˈtɪʃn]

考试 KET/PET/IELTS/TOEFL/
PTE
科目 all

We are in competition with four other companies for the contract.

我们在与其他四家公司竞争这项合同。

competitive

竞争的；好竞争的；（价格等的）有竞争力的

adj. [kəmˈpetətɪv]

考试 KET/PET/IELTS/TOEFL/
PTE
科目 all

Graduates have to fight for jobs in a highly competitive market.

毕业生不得不在竞争激烈的市场上奋力争取找到工作。

complain

抱怨；申诉

v. [kəmˈpleɪn]

考试 KET/PET/IELTS/TOEFL/
PTE
科目 all

He complained bitterly that he had been unfairly treated.

他愤懑地诉说他所受到的不公平待遇。

complement

补充物，补足物；足数，足额；补语

n. [ˈkɒmplɪmənt]

考试 TOEFL/IELTS/PTE
科目 listening

Homework is a necessary complement to classroom study.

家庭作业是课堂学习的必要补充。

C

complete

整个的，全部的；完全的，圆满的

adj. [kəmˈpliːt]

考试 KET/PET/IELTS/TOEFL/PTE
科目 all

You will receive payment for each complete day that you work.

你将按你每一整天的工作领取报酬。

完成，结束；使完整

vt. [kəmˈpliːt]

考试 KET/PET/IELTS/TOEFL/PTE
科目 all

The project will be completed by the end of October.

这项工程将于 10 月底竣工。

complicate

使……复杂；使……难懂；使（疾病等）恶化

vt. [ˈkɒmplɪkeɪt]

考试 TOEFL/IELTS
科目 writing

The issue is complicated by the fact that a vital document is missing.

一份重要文件的遗失使这个问题复杂化了。

comply

遵从，照做，应允；顺从，服从

vi. [kəmˈplaɪ]

考试 TOEFL/IELTS
科目 writing

Companies that do not comply may lose their assets and operating licences.

那些不遵从规定的公司可能会失去资产和营业执照。

compose

组成，构成；创作；撰写；使平静

v. [kəmˈpəʊz]

考试 TOEFL/IELTS
科目 writing

Emma frowned, making an effort to compose herself.

艾玛皱起了眉头，努力使自己镇定下来。

comprehensive

内容广泛的，总括性的；综合的；所有的

adj. [ˌkɒmprɪˈhensɪv]

The reporter has made a comprehensive report.

记者已做了全面的报道。

compromise

妥协，折中

n. [ˈkɒmprəmaɪz]

After lengthy talks the two sides finally reached a compromise.

双方经过长期的商谈终于达成了妥协。

compulsory

义务的；强制的

adj. [kəmˈpʌlsəri]

It is compulsory for all motorcyclists to wear helmets.

所有骑摩托的人都必须戴头盔，这是强制性的。

conceal

隐藏，隐蔽

vt. [kənˈsiːl]

Many people choose to conceal or alter their identity online.

许多人选择在网络世界隐藏或改变自己的身份。

concede

(不情愿地) 承认，承认……属实 (或正确)；让与

vt. [kənˈsiːd]

The president was obliged to concede power to the army.

总统被迫把权力让给军队。

conceive

想出（主意等）；怀孕

v. ［kənˈsiːv］

考试 TOEFL/IELTS
科目 writing

He conceived the idea of transforming the old power station into an arts center.
他想出了一个把旧发电站改造成艺术中心的主意。

concentrate

集中；全神贯注于；（使）浓缩

v. ［ˈkɒnsntreɪt］

考试 KET/PET/IELTS/TOEFL/PTE
科目 all

We need to concentrated resources on the most run-down areas.
我们需要把资源集中用于最衰败的地区。

浓缩物

n. ［ˈkɒnsntreɪt］

考试 KET/PET/IELTS/TOEFL/PTE
科目 all

The lemon juice is the mixture of concentrate and water.
柠檬汁是由浓缩的柠檬素和水混合而成的。

concentration

集中；专注；浓缩

n. ［ˌkɒnsnˈtreɪʃn］

考试 KET/PET/IELTS/TOEFL/PTE
科目 all

Stress and tiredness affect your powers of concentration.
紧张和疲劳影响注意力的集中。

concept

概念，观念，设想

n. ［ˈkɒnsept］

考试 KET/PET/IELTS/TOEFL/PTE
科目 all

He presented a new concept of the beginning of the universe.
他提出了一种宇宙起源的新概念。

concert

音乐会，演奏会；和谐，一致

n. [ˈkɒnsət]

考试 KET/PET/IELTS/TOEFL/PTE
科目 all

The concert was criticized by some exile groups in the United States.

此次音乐会招致了一些流亡美国人的指责。

conclude

结束，终止；断定，下结论；缔结，达成

v. [kənˈkluːd]

考试 KET/PET/IELTS/TOEFL/PTE
科目 all

I would like to conclude with a sad, but true, story from my childhood.

我想以童年时一个悲伤但真实的故事结束我的演讲。

conclusion

结论，推论；结尾；缔结，达成

n. [kənˈkluːʒn]

考试 KET/PET/IELTS/TOEFL/PTE
科目 all

The conclusion was deduced from the premises.

这个结论是由前提推断出来的。

concrete

有形的；具体的

adj. [ˈkɒŋkriːt]

考试 TOEFL/IELTS/PTE
科目 listening

It is easier to think in concrete terms rather than in the abstract.

结合具体的事物来思考要比抽象思考容易些。

concur

同意，赞同

v. [kənˈkɜː(r)]

考试 TOEFL/IELTS
科目 writing

Historians have concurred with each other in this view.

历史学家在这个观点上已达成一致。

condense

冷凝，凝结；精简，浓缩

v. ［kənˈdens］

考试 TOEFL/IELTS
科目 writing

Steam condenses into water when it cools.
蒸汽冷却时凝结为水。

condition

条件，状况；环境

n. ［kənˈdɪʃn］

考试 KET/PET/IELTS/TOEFL/
PTE
科目 all

The plants grow best in cool, damp conditions.
这些植物最适合在阴凉潮湿的环境下生长。

训练；使习惯于；影响（某事发生的方式）

vt. ［kənˈdɪʃən］

考试 KET/PET/IELTS/TOEFL/
PTE
科目 all

Gender roles are often conditioned by cultural factors.
文化因素常常对性别角色有着重要的影响。

conduce

导致；有助于

vi. ［kənˈdjuːs］

考试 TOEFL/IELTS
科目 writing

Money and beauty do not always conduce to happiness.
金钱与美丽未必一定会带来幸福。

conducive

有益于……的，有助于……的

adj. ［kənˈdjuːsɪv］

考试 TOEFL/IELTS/PTE
科目 reading

Noisy conditions aren't really conducive to concentrated work.
嘈杂的环境实在不利于专心工作。

conduct

行为，举止

n. [ˈkɒndʌkt]

考试 TOEFL/IELTS/PTE
科目 reading

The sport has a strict code of conduct.
体育运动有着严格的行为规范。

confer

协商；授予

v. [kənˈfɜː(r)]

考试 TOEFL/IELTS
科目 writing

An honorary degree was conferred on him by Oxford University in 1995.
牛津大学于 1995 年授予他荣誉学位。

confide

委托；吐露秘密

v. [kənˈfaɪd]

考试 TOEFL/IELTS
科目 writing

It is important to have someone you can confide in.
有一位心腹知己很重要。

confidence

信任；信心，自信；秘密，机密

n. [ˈkɒnfɪdəns]

考试 KET/PET/IELTS/TOEFL/PTE
科目 all

While girls lack confidence, boys often overestimate their abilities.
虽然女孩经常缺乏自信，但男孩往往高估自己的能力。

confident

自信的；确信的，有把握的

adj. [ˈkɒnfɪdənt]

考试 KET/PET/IELTS/TOEFL/PTE
科目 all

Being confident comes with feeling good about yourself.
当你自我感觉良好时，自信会随之而来。

confine

限制；禁闭；使离不开（或受困于床、轮椅等）

vt. [kənˈfaɪn]

考试 TOEFL/IELTS/PTE
科目 listening

He was confined to a wheelchair after the accident.
经过那场事故后，他就离不开轮椅了。

conform

相符合；遵从；顺从

vi. [kənˈfɔːm]

考试 TOEFL/IELTS
科目 writing

He refused to conform to the local customs.
他拒绝遵从当地的风俗习惯。

confront

使面对，面临

vt. [kənˈfrʌnt]

考试 TOEFL/IELTS/PTE
科目 listening

Most people when confronted with a horse will pat it.
大多数人遇见马时都会轻轻地拍拍它。

confuse

使困惑；混淆

vt. [kənˈfjuːz]

考试 KET/PET/IELTS/TOEFL/PTE
科目 all

His comments only served to confuse the issue further.
他的评论只是把问题弄得更加复杂了。

congratulate

祝贺，向……道贺

vt. [kənˈɡrætʃuleɪt]

考试 KET/PET/IELTS/TOEFL/PTE
科目 all

You can congratulate yourself on having done a good job.
你的工作做得很出色，你应该感到自豪。

congratulation

祝贺；贺辞

n. [kənˌgrætʃuˈleɪʃn]

考试 KET/PET/IELTS/TOEFL/
PTE
科目 all

Please add my warmest congratulations to the large chorus of friends acclaiming your graduation.
请把我最热烈的祝贺汇入朋友们给你的毕业赞歌。

connect

连接；与……联系；接通（电话）；衔接；联运；建立良好关系；沟通

v. [kəˈnekt]

考试 KET/PET/IELTS/TOEFL/
PTE
科目 all

The canal was built to connect Sheffield with the Humber estuary.
修建这条运河是为了将谢菲尔德和亨伯河河口连接起来。
They met a couple of times but they didn't really connect.
尽管他们见了几次面，但仍未真正建立起良好的关系。

connection

联系，连接；亲戚，社会关系；转车

n. [kəˈnekʃn]

考试 KET/PET/IELTS/TOEFL/
PTE
科目 all

There are good bus and train connections between the resort and major cities.
在这处旅游胜地和主要城市之间有着便利的公交车和火车运输。

conscience

良心，良知；内疚，愧疚

n. [ˈkɒnʃəns]

考试 TOEFL/IELTS/PTE
科目 listening

Don't let the fear of rejection pressure you to sin against your own conscience.
不要让被人拒绝的恐惧所产生的压力迫使你违背自己的良心。

C

consequence

结果，后果，影响；重要性

n. [ˈkɒnsɪkwəns]

考试 TOEFL/IELTS/PTE
科目 reading

Maternity services were to be reduced in consequence of falling birth rates.

由于出生率下降，产科服务会随之削减。

conservation

保存，保护，保持

n. [ˌkɒnsəˈveɪʃn]

考试 KET/PET/IELTS/TOEFL/PTE
科目 all

Indian government has intervened on issues ranging from forest conservation to bus fuel.

印度政府对从森林保护到公共汽车燃料等问题都进行了干预。

consider

考虑，细想；体谅，顾及；认为，把……看作

v. [kənˈsɪdə(r)]

考试 KET/PET/IELTS/TOEFL/PTE
科目 all

We need to consider how the law might be reformed.

我们得斟酌法律应该如何修订。

considerate

考虑周到的，体谅的

adj. [kənˈsɪdərət]

考试 TOEFL/IELTS/PTE
科目 reading

Courtesy is respecting our differences, being considerate of each other's feelings, and being patient with people who irritate us.

礼貌是尊重彼此的差异、体贴别人的感受、容忍激怒我们的人。

consideration

需要考虑的事；理由；考虑，思考；照顾

n. [kənˌsɪdəˈreɪʃn]

考试 TOEFL/IELTS/PTE
科目 listening

Protective benefits are the primary consideration for consumers.

保护自身利益是消费者考虑的首要因素。

consist

组成，存在

vi. ［kən'sɪst］

考试 TOEFL/IELTS/PTE
科目 listening

Intellectual property consists of a bundle of rights governing products of the intellect.

知识产权包括一系列与智力产品相关的权利。

consolidate

使巩固，使加强；把……合为一体

v. ［kən'sɒlɪdeɪt］

考试 TOEFL/IELTS
科目 writing

The authorities are trying to consolidate security with legality and infrastructure.

有关当局正试图通过合法途径和基础建设来巩固治安。

conspicuous

明显的，引人注目的

adj. ［kən'spɪkjuəs］

考试 TOEFL/IELTS/PTE
科目 reading

The advertisements were all posted in a conspicuous place.

广告都贴在了显眼的地方。

constitute

组成，构成，形成；设立，建立

vt. ［'kɒnstɪtjuːt］

考试 TOEFL/IELTS/PTE
科目 reading

The committee was constituted in 1974 by an Act of Parliament.

该委员会是根据一项议会法案于 1974 年设立的。

construct

建设，建造，构造；创立

vt. ［kən'strʌkt］

考试 TOEFL/IELTS/PTE
科目 listening

Australia's plans mean it will join a global race to construct the world's biggest solar plant.

澳大利亚的计划意味着它将投身于建造全球最大太阳能电厂的国际竞争。

construe

理解，领会

vt. ［kənˈstruː］

考试 TOEFL/IELTS
科目 writing

Her words could hardly be construed as an apology.

她的话怎么想都不像是道歉。

consume

消耗，吃完，喝光；使着迷；烧毁

vt. ［kənˈsjuːm］

考试 TOEFL/IELTS/PTE
科目 listening

He consumed much time and energy in writing this book.

他写这本书消耗了很多时间和精力。

contact

接触；联络；会见；熟人；（电流的）接通

n. ［ˈkɒntækt］

考试 KET/PET/IELTS/TOEFL/
PTE
科目 all

The switches close the contacts and complete the circuit.

这些开关可接通形成闭合电路。

联系，联络（如用电话或信件）

vt. ［ˈkɒntækt］

考试 KET/PET/IELTS/TOEFL/
PTE
科目 all

If you have any problem, contact the tour conductor.

如果你有任何难题，请与旅行团向导联系。

contain

包含，容纳；容忍，抑制；防止……蔓延（或恶化）

v. ［kənˈteɪn］

考试 KET/PET/IELTS/TOEFL/
PTE
科目 all

The planned building for the site will contain offices and some retail stores.

该地块上计划修建的建筑物将包括写字楼和一些零售店。

contemporary

同时代的，当代的

adj. [kənˈtemprəri]

考试 TOEFL/IELTS/PTE
科目 reading

Contemporary culture changes like shifting sands.
现代文化的日益更新如同流沙。

content

内容；目录

n. [ˈkɒntent]

考试 KET/PET/IELTS/TOEFL/
PTE
科目 all

You tone of voice is as important as the content of what you have to say.
你讲话的声调和你要讲的内容同样重要。

使满意（足）

vt. [kənˈtent]

考试 KET/PET/IELTS/TOEFL/
PTE
科目 all

Her apology seemed to content him.
她的道歉好像使他感到满意了。

context

背景，环境；上下文

n. [ˈkɒntekst]

考试 TOEFL/IELTS/PTE
科目 listening

Your research topic needs to be located in its context and background.
你的研究主题需要处于一定的语境和背景之中。

continue

继续，持续；延伸

v. [kənˈtɪnjuː]

考试 KET/PET/IELTS/TOEFL/
PTE
科目 all

The path continued over rough, rocky ground.
这条小路继续穿过崎岖不平的石头地面。

contradict

反驳，否认；与……矛盾

vt. [ˌkɒntrəˈdɪkt]

考试 TOEFL/IELTS/PTE
科目 listening

When existing provisions concerning marine environmental protection contradict this law, this law shall prevail.

现行的有关海洋环境保护的规定，凡与本法抵触的，均以本法为准。

contrast

对比；形成对照

v. [kənˈtrɑːst]

考试 TOEFL/IELTS
科目 writing

It is interesting to contrast the British legal system with the American one.

把英国的法律制度与美国的法律制度加以对比很有意思。

contribution

贡献；捐款，捐献物；投稿

n. [ˌkɒntrɪˈbjuːʃn]

考试 TOEFL/IELTS/PTE
科目 reading

The emerging world will undoubtedly make a growing contribution to breakthrough innovations.

新兴市场无疑将会对突破性的创新做出越来越大的贡献。

control

控制，支配

n. [kənˈtrəʊl]

考试 KET/PET/IELTS/TOEFL/PTE
科目 all

Owing to circumstances beyond our control, the flight to Rome has been cancelled.

由于出现了我们无法控制的情况，这趟飞往罗马的航班已被取消。

控制，支配

vt. [kənˈtrəʊl]

考试 KET/PET/IELTS/TOEFL/PTE
科目 all

Her voice was beginning to rise and she tried in vain to control it.

她的音量开始提高，她试图控制住，但做不到。

controversy

争论，辩论，争吵

n. [ˈkɒntrəvɜːsi]

考试 TOEFL/IELTS/PTE
科目 reading

The president resigned amid considerable controversy.

总统在一片争论声中辞职了。

convenience

便利；便利的设施

n. [kənˈviːniəns]

考试 KET/PET/IELTS/TOEFL/
PTE
科目 all

Our focus is to bring convenience and enjoyment to our customers.

我们关注的焦点是为客户带来便利和享受。

convenient

便利的，方便的

adj. [kənˈviːniənt]

考试 KET/PET/IELTS/TOEFL/
PTE
科目 all

Convenient，cheaper deliveries will encourage more people to shop online.

便捷实惠的送货方式将鼓励更多的人在网上购物。

convention

会议；协定；惯例；习俗

n. [kənˈvenʃn]

考试 TOEFL/IELTS/PTE
科目 listening

I made arrangements to meet him on the plaza outside our convention center.

我安排好了跟他在会议中心外面的广场上见面。

conventional

惯例的，常规的；传统的

adj. [kənˈvenʃənl]

考试 TOEFL/IELTS/PTE
科目 reading

Nowadays plastics have taken the place of many conventional materials.

现在，塑胶已经代替了许多传统材料。

C

conversation

会话，谈话

n. [ˌkɒnvəˈseɪʃn]

考试 KET/PET/IELTS/TOEFL/PTE
科目 all

The main topic of conversation was the probable outcome of the election.

谈话的主题是选举可能产生的结果。

convert

转变；兑换；使改变信仰

vt. [kənˈvɜːt]

考试 TOEFL/IELTS/PTE
科目 listening

We've converted from coal to gas central heating.

我们已由燃煤改换成燃气集中供暖。

convey

运送；转达，传达

vt. [kənˈveɪ]

考试 TOEFL/IELTS/PTE
科目 reading

Pipes convey hot water from the boiler to the radiators.

管道把热水从锅炉输送到暖气片。

cooperate

协作，合作

vi. [kəʊˈɒpəreɪt]

考试 TOEFL/IELTS/PTE
科目 reading

The company will cooperate with any government probe in the matter.

该公司将全力配合任何政府部门对该事件的调查。

cope

竞争，对抗；对付，妥善处理

vi. [kəʊp]

考试 TOEFL/IELTS/PTE
科目 reading

Desert plants are adapted to cope with extreme heat.

沙漠植物适于耐酷热。

core

果核；中心，核心

n. [kɔː(r)]

考试 KET/PET/IELTS/TOEFL/PTE
科目 all

Concern for the environment is at the core of our policies.

对环境的关注是我们政策的中心。

---

corn

谷物，庄稼，玉米

n. [kɔːn]

考试 KET/PET/IELTS/TOEFL/PTE
科目 all

They are meditating a reimposition of the tax on corn.

他们正在考虑对谷物重新征税。

---

corner

角落，拐角

n. ['kɔːnə(r)]

考试 KET/PET/IELTS/TOEFL/PTE
科目 all

Write your address in the top right-hand corner of the letter.

把你的地址写在信的右上角。

---

corporate

社团的；公司的；组成公司（团体）的，法人的；共同的

adj. ['kɔːpərət]

考试 TOEFL/IELTS/PTE
科目 listening

The law applies to both individuals and corporate bodies.

本法律适用于个人和法人团体。

---

correctly

正确地，恰当地

adv. [kə'rektli]

考试 KET/PET/IELTS/TOEFL/PTE
科目 all

If I remember correctly, the lecture was cancelled.

如果我没记错的话，那次演讲取消了。

C

correlate

（使）相互关联影响；相互依赖；显示……的紧密联系

v. [ˈkɒrəleɪt]

考试 TOEFL/IELTS
科目 writing

A high-fat diet correlates with a greater risk of heart disease.

高脂肪饮食与增加心脏病发作的风险密切相关。

cottage

村舍，小屋，别墅

n. [ˈkɒtɪdʒ]

考试 KET/PET/IELTS/TOEFL/PTE
科目 all

The cottage is tiny, but it's charming.

这间小屋虽小，却十分迷人。

cotton

棉花；棉线，棉纱；棉制品

n. [ˈkɒtn]

考试 KET/PET/IELTS/TOEFL/PTE
科目 all

The building stands as the last remaining relic of the town's cotton industry.

这座建筑物是小镇棉纺业仅存的遗迹。

count

数数；计算；算入；看作，认为

v. [kaʊnt]

考试 KET/PET/IELTS/TOEFL/PTE
科目 all

I count him among my closest friends.

我把他看作我最亲密的朋友之一。

计数，总数

n. [kaʊnt]

考试 KET/PET/IELTS/TOEFL/PTE
科目 all

The bus driver did a quick count of the empty seats.

公共汽车司机很快地数了数空位。

counterpart

对应的事物或人

n. [ˈkaʊntəpɑːt]

考试 TOEFL/IELTS/PTE
科目 reading

It is not a unique instance, but has its counterpart.

无独有偶。

couple

（一）对，双；夫妇

n. [ˈkʌpl]

考试 KET/PET/IELTS/TOEFL/ PTE
科目 all

I saw a couple of men get out.

我看见两个男人出去了。

连接，结合

v. [ˈkʌpl]

考试 KET/PET/IELTS/TOEFL/ PTE
科目 all

The two train cars has been coupled together.

两节火车车厢已经挂上钩了。

courage

勇气，胆量

n. [ˈkʌrɪdʒ]

考试 KET/PET/IELTS/TOEFL/ PTE
科目 all

He showed great courage and determination.

他表现得十分勇敢和果断。

course

过程；路线；课程

n. [kɔːs]

考试 KET/PET/IELTS/TOEFL/ PTE
科目 all

The college runs specialist language courses.

这所学院开设了专门的语言课程。

courteous

有礼貌的

adj. [ˈkɜːtiəs]

考试 TOEFL/IELTS/PTE
科目 listening

The hotel staff are friendly and courteous.

旅馆服务人员友好而有礼貌。

C

courtyard

院子，庭院；天井

n. [ˈkɔːtjɑːd]

考试 KET/PET/IELTS/TOEFL/
PTE
科目 all

We went through a stone archway into the courtyard.
我们穿过石拱门进入了院子。

craftsmanship

手艺，技艺；精工细作

n. [ˈkrɑːftsmənʃɪp]

考试 TOEFL/IELTS/PTE
科目 listening

We admired the superb craftsmanship of the furniture.
我们很欣赏这件家具的一流工艺。

crash

撞车，相撞；突然坠落；倒闭；碰撞声，破裂声

n. [kræʃ]

考试 KET/PET/IELTS/TOEFL/
PTE
科目 all

A girl was killed yesterday in a crash involving a stolen car.
昨天，有一个女孩在一桩涉及窃车的撞车事故中丧生。

坠毁，碰撞，冲过；（公司）倒闭

v. [kræʃ]

考试 KET/PET/IELTS/TOEFL/
PTE
科目 all

A truck went out of control and crashed into the back of a bus.
货车失控撞上了一辆公共汽车的尾部。

crave

渴望；恳求

v. [kreɪv]

考试 TOEFL/IELTS
科目 writing

Many young children crave (for) attention.
许多小孩子渴望得到关心。

crazy

疯狂的，古怪的；愚蠢的；狂热的

adj. [ˈkreɪzɪ]

考试 KET/PET/IELTS/TOEFL/
PTE
科目 all

There were a lot of crazy, dangerous people in the street.

街上有很多狂热的、危险的人。

create

创造，创作；引起，造成；建立

vt. [kriˈeɪt]

考试 KET/PET/IELTS/TOEFL/
PTE
科目 all

We learned how to create and register a new web page.

我们学会了新网页的制作和注册方法。

creation

创造；创作；创造物

n. [kriˈeɪʃn]

考试 KET/PET/IELTS/TOEFL/
PTE
科目 all

Job creation has become an imperative for the government.

创造就业机会是政府必须做的事。

creative

有创造力的，创造性的

adj. [kriˈeɪtɪv]

考试 TOEFL/IELTS/PTE
科目 listening

Creative thinking is the antecedence of design.

要想做出创新性设计，必须先有创新性思维。

credit

信誉，信用

n. [ˈkredɪt]

考试 TOEFL/IELTS/PTE
科目 reading

The firm's credit has been badly shaken.

这家公司的信誉已大大受损。

crime

罪行，犯罪

n. ［kraɪm］

考试 KET/PET/IELTS/TOEFL/PTE
科目 all

The brutality of the crime has appalled the public.
罪行之残暴使公众大为震惊。

critical

危急的；批评的，苛求的；关键的

adj. ［ˈkrɪtɪkl］

考试 TOEFL/IELTS/PTE
科目 reading

Reducing levels of carbon dioxide in the atmosphere is of critical importance.
减少大气层中的二氧化碳含量极其重要。

crossroads

交叉路口，十字路口

n. ［ˈkrɒsrəʊdz］

考试 KET/PET/IELTS/TOEFL/PTE
科目 all

The world is at a crossroads, with popular expectations diverging from reality.
世界正处在十字路口，而民众的期望值与现实相去甚远。

crowd

人群；一群，一伙

n. ［kraʊd］

考试 KET/PET/IELTS/TOEFL/PTE
科目 all

I squeezed carefully through the crowd.
我小心翼翼地挤过了这群人。

聚集，群集；挤满，拥挤

v. ［kraʊd］

考试 KET/PET/IELTS/TOEFL/PTE
科目 all

We all crowded around the stove to keep warm.
我们都挤在炉边取暖。

crown

王冠；王权；顶部

n. ［kraʊn］

考试 KET/PET/IELTS/TOEFL/ PTE
科目 all

Taking off the crown she is still the princess.

摘掉王冠后，她依然是公主。

为……加冕；褒奖；给……加顶；使圆满

vt. ［kraʊn］

考试 KET/PET/IELTS/TOEFL/ PTE
科目 all

Elizabeth was crowned in Westminster Abbey on 2 June 1953.

伊丽莎白于 1953 年 6 月 2 日在威斯敏斯特大教堂加冕。

crude

天然的；粗鲁的；粗制的

adj. ［kruːd］

考试 KET/PET/IELTS/TOEFL/ PTE
科目 all

The plant converts crude oil into gasoline.

这家工厂将原油加工成汽油。

cruel

残忍的，残酷的

adj. ［ˈkruːəl］

考试 KET/PET/IELTS/TOEFL/ PTE
科目 all

I can't stand people who are cruel to animals.

我无法容忍虐待动物的人。

cultivate

耕作，种植，栽培；培养；发展

vt. ［ˈkʌltɪveɪt］

考试 TOEFL/IELTS/PTE
科目 reading

We should cultivate the good habits of diligence and frugality.

我们要养成勤俭节约的好习惯。

culture

文化；养殖

n. ［ˈkʌltʃə(r)］

考试 KET/PET/IELTS/TOEFL/ PTE
科目 all

Just like spoken language, body language varies from culture to culture.

就像口头语言一样，身势语也因文化的不同而有所差异。

C

curiosity

好奇心；奇物，珍品

n. [ˌkjʊəriˈɒsəti]

考试 TOEFL/IELTS/PTE
科目 reading

He had an insatiable curiosity about a wide variety of issues.
他对各种各样的事情都有一种从不满足的好奇心。

curious

好奇的，爱打听的

adj. [ˈkjʊəriəs]

考试 TOEFL/IELTS/PTE
科目 listening

The reporter is curious to know whether the official is involved in the case.
这名记者很想知道那位官员是否涉及此案。

当前的；流通的

adj. [ˈkʌrənt]

考试 KET/PET/IELTS/TOEFL/PTE
科目 all

The current situation is very different to that in 1990.
当前的形势与 1990 年截然不同。

currently

现时；当前；目前；当下

adv. [ˈkʌrəntli]

考试 KET/PET/IELTS/TOEFL/PTE
科目 all

All the options are currently available.
所有的方案现在均可选择。

curtain

窗帘，门帘；幕（布）；结束

n. [ˈkɜːtn]

考试 KET/PET/IELTS/TOEFL/PTE
科目 all

There was tremendous applause when the curtain came down.
幕落时响起了经久不息的掌声。

curve

曲线；弧线；弯曲

n. ［kɜːv］

考试 KET/PET/IELTS/TOEFL/PTE
科目 all

The driver lost control on a curve and the vehicle hit a tree.

司机在拐弯处失控，车撞在了一棵树上。

customer

顾客，主顾

n. ［ˈkʌstəmə(r)］

考试 KET/PET/IELTS/TOEFL/PTE
科目 all

The customer was impressed by the machine's performance.

客户对机器的良好性能很满意。

cutting

锋利的；尖刻的

adj. ［ˈkʌtɪŋ］

考试 TOEFL/IELTS/PTE
科目 listening

People make cutting remarks to help themselves feel superior or powerful.

人们说话尖酸刻薄是为了使自己感觉高高在上或是有权有势。

cycle

自行车；循环，周期

n. ［ˈsaɪkl］

考试 KET/PET/IELTS/TOEFL/PTE
科目 all

This is a calendar based on both lunar and solar cycles.

这是基于日月周期的历法。

骑自行车；循环

vi. ［ˈsaɪkl］

考试 TOEFL/IELTS/PTE
科目 listening

People willing to walk or cycle can navigate 75 kilometers of upgraded routes in the region.

喜欢步行或者骑自行车的人可以在这一地区新修的75公里的路上通行。

D

daily

考试 KET/PET/IELTS/TOEFL/
PTE
科目 all

日报

n. [ˈdeɪli]

You are welcome to share your stories with *China Daily* website readers.

欢迎您来与《中国日报》网站的读者分享您的故事。

dam

考试 KET/PET/IELTS/TOEFL/
PTE
科目 all

水坝，拦河坝

n. [dæm]

Once operational, the dam will produce the energy of 15 nuclear power plants.

大坝一旦投入使用，将会产生相当于 15 座核电站发出的电量。

damage

考试 KET/PET/IELTS/TOEFL/
PTE
科目 all

损害

vt. [ˈdæmɪdʒ]

The paintwork was damaged when my car hit the gate.

我的汽车撞上了大门，汽车的漆面被弄坏了。

损害，毁坏；损害赔偿金

n. [ˈdæmɪdʒ]

考试 KET/PET/IELTS/TOEFL/
PTE
科目 all

Many professional boxers end their careers with brain damage.

许多职业拳击手结束运动生涯时都已受到了脑损伤。

He was vindicated in court and damages were awarded.

他在法庭上被证明无罪，并且获得了损害赔偿金。

damp

潮湿的

adj. [dæmp]

考试 TOEFL/IELTS/PTE
科目 listening

Keeping vegetables in slightly damp sand has been a storage method for many centuries.

将蔬菜存放在稍微潮湿的沙子里面是多年以来的蔬菜存储方法。

danger

危险；威胁；危险事物

n. ['deɪndʒə(r)]

考试 KET/PET/IELTS/TOEFL/PTE
科目 all

Children's lives are in danger every time they cross this road.

孩子们每次过这条马路时都面临着危险。

dangerous

危险的，不安全的

adj. ['deɪndʒərəs]

考试 KET/PET/IELTS/TOEFL/PTE
科目 all

We argued him out of going on such a dangerous journey.

我们劝他别参加如此危险的旅行。

Danish

丹麦的

adj. ['deɪnɪʃ]

考试 KET/PET/IELTS/TOEFL/PTE
科目 all

The Danish medical association accused politicians of putting the economy before public health.

丹麦医学协会指责政治家们把经济放在公共卫生之上。

丹麦人

n. ['deɪnɪʃ]

考试 KET/PET/IELTS/TOEFL/PTE
科目 all

He was the son of a Danish father and a Venezuelan mother.

他的父亲是丹麦人，母亲是委内瑞拉人。

D

Denmark

丹麦

n. ['denmɑːk]

考试 KET/PET/IELTS/TOEFL/PTE
科目 all

Denmark has ruled Greenland since the 18th century.

自从 18 世纪起，格陵兰就成了丹麦的属地。

dare

敢；挑战；竟敢

v. [deə(r)]

考试 KET/PET/IELTS/TOEFL/PTE
科目 all

The gymnast dared a breathtakingly difficult move.

这名体操选手敢于做惊险的高难度动作。

daring

大胆的，勇敢的

adj. ['deərɪŋ]

考试 KET/PET/IELTS/TOEFL/PTE
科目 all

Daring modern architecture proclaimed that London was a true world city.

设计大胆的现代建筑正式宣告伦敦成为一个真正的国际性城市。

darkness

黑暗

n. ['dɑːknəs]

考试 KET/PET/IELTS/TOEFL/PTE
科目 all

An almost full moon illuminates the darkness.

月近圆满，照亮了黑暗。

data

资料，数据

n. ['deɪtə]

考试 KET/PET/IELTS/TOEFL/PTE
科目 all

A lot more government data are being made public.

更多的政府资料将公之于众。

date

注明……的日期

v. [deɪt]

考试 KET/PET/IELTS/TOEFL/PTE
科目 all

Once the decision is reached, he can date and sign the sheet.

一旦决议达成，他就可以在这张纸上签署日期和姓名了。

约会

n. [deɪt]

考试 KET/PET/IELTS/TOEFL/PTE
科目 all

He made a date with the girl he had met the day before.

他和前一天遇到的那个女孩定下了约会。

daylight

日光；白昼；黎明

n. ['deɪlaɪt]

考试 KET/PET/IELTS/TOEFL/PTE
科目 all

Lack of daylight can make people feel depressed.

日晒不足会让人情绪低落。

daytime

白天，日间

n. ['deɪtaɪm]

考试 KET/PET/IELTS/TOEFL/PTE
科目 all

Bats sleep in the daytime and come out to hunt for food at night.

蝙蝠白天睡觉，夜里才出来寻觅食物。

dazzle

使眼花，使目眩；使迷惑；使赞叹不已

v. ['dæzl]

考试 TOEFL/IELTS/PTE
科目 listening

I was dazzled by the spotlights as I walked onto the stage.

当我走上舞台时，被聚光灯照得睁不开眼睛。

deaf

聋的，不愿听的

adj. ［def］

考试 KET/PET/IELTS/TOEFL/ PTE
科目 all

Scientists have long known that deaf or blind people have heightened senses outside of their impairment.

科学家一直都知道，失聪或失明的人提高了受损感官以外的感觉。

deafen

使聋；使隔音

vt. ［ˈdefn］

考试 TOEFL/IELTS
科目 writing

Texting on your mobile phone while crossing the road might deafen your ears to the sound of an approaching car.

过马路时边走边发短信，你就很容易忽略正在靠近的汽车的声音。

deal

处理；做买卖，经营；分配；对待

v. ［diːl］

考试 KET/PET/IELTS/TOEFL/ PTE
科目 all

She is used to dealing with all kinds of people in her job.

她已经习惯于和工作中遇到的各种各样的人打交道。

交易

n. ［diːl］

考试 KET/PET/IELTS/TOEFL/ PTE
科目 all

Corporate sponsors are convinced they get a good deal.

公司赞助商确信他们做的是一桩好买卖。

debate

争论，辩论

v. ［dɪˈbeɪt］

考试 KET/PET/IELTS/TOEFL/ PTE
科目 all

The committee will debate whether to lower the age of club membership to 16.

委员会将讨论是否将参加俱乐部的年龄限制放宽到 16 岁。

争论，辩论

n. [dɪˈbeɪt]

考试 KET/PET/IELTS/TOEFL/PTE
科目 all

The theatre's future is a subject of considerable debate.

剧院的前途是一个颇具争议的问题。

decade

十年

n. [ˈdekeɪd]

考试 KET/PET/IELTS/TOEFL/PTE
科目 all

The rate of foreign investment has soared around tenfold in the past decade.

外国投资的比率在过去十年中增加了大约 10 倍。

deceitful

不诚实的，骗人的

v. [dɪˈsiːtfl]

考试 TOEFL/IELTS
科目 writing

I advise you not to cooperate with that deceitful businessman.

我建议你不要和那个不诚实的商人合作。

decent

正当的；合适的，得体的；尚可的

adj. [ˈdiːsnt]

考试 TOEFL/IELTS/PTE
科目 reading

The lack of decent public transport is a great disadvantage.

没有适当的公共交通工具是很不方便的。

decide

决定，下决心；解决，裁决

v. [dɪˈsaɪd]

考试 KET/PET/IELTS/TOEFL/PTE
科目 all

A mixture of skill and good luck decided the outcome of the game.

技术和运气结合在一起决定了比赛的结果。

decided

明显的，明白无误的

adj. ［dɪˈsaɪdɪd］

考试 KET/PET/IELTS/TOEFL/PTE
科目 all

He's a man of very decided opinions.
他是个态度鲜明的人。

decision

决定，决心；决议，决策

n. ［dɪˈsɪʒn］

考试 KET/PET/IELTS/TOEFL/PTE
科目 all

We must come to a decision about what to do next by tomorrow.
我们最晚在明天必须就下一步做什么做出决定。

decisive

决定性的；果断的，决断的

adj. ［dɪˈsaɪsɪv］

考试 TOEFL/IELTS/PTE
科目 listening

He should give way to a younger, more decisive leader.
他应该让位于更年轻、更有决断力的领导者。

decompose

分解；腐败，腐烂

v. ［ˌdiːkəmˈpəʊz］

考试 TOEFL/IELTS
科目 writing

The microbes decompose the organic matter, using up the oxygen.
微生物分解有机物需要氧气。

decrease

减小，减少

v. ［dɪˈkriːs］

考试 KET/PET/IELTS/TOEFL/PTE
科目 all

Good posture can improve your running efficiency and decrease injury risk.
保持良好的形体能提高你跑步的效率，降低受伤的概率。

减少量

n. [ˈdiːkriːs]

考试 KET/PET/IELTS/TOEFL/
PTE
科目 all

The decrease in sales was almost 20 percent.

销售量差不多减少了 20%。

D

deduct

（从总量中）扣除，减去

vt. [dɪˈdʌkt]

考试 TOEFL/IELTS/PTE
科目 listening

The cost of your uniform will be deducted from your wages.

制服费将从你的工资中扣除。

defeat

击败，使失败；困住，难住，使困惑

vt. [dɪˈfiːt]

考试 KET/PET/IELTS/TOEFL/
PTE
科目 all

The instruction manual completely defeated me.

这份操作指南把我完全弄糊涂了。

击败，失败

n. [dɪˈfiːt]

考试 KET/PET/IELTS/TOEFL/
PTE
科目 all

The world champion has only had two defeats in 20 fights.

这位世界冠军在 20 场拳击赛中只输过两场。

deficient

缺乏的；欠缺的

adj. [dɪˈfɪʃnt]

考试 TOEFL/IELTS/PTE
科目 listening

They are sometimes treated as being mentally deficient.

他们有时被看作智力不健全的人。

define

给……下定义；阐述，阐释；限定，规定

v. [dɪˈfaɪn]

考试 TOEFL/IELTS/PTE
科目 reading

Sex is the biological and physiological characteristics that define male and female.

性别是用来界定男性和女性生物及生理特征的。

definitive

最后的；可靠的，权威的；决定性的；不可更改的

adj. [dɪˈfɪnətɪv]

考试 TOEFL/IELTS/PTE
科目 reading

The definitive version of the text is ready to be published.

正式的文本很快就要发表了。

degree

程度；度数；学位；等级

n. [dɪˈɡriː]

考试 KET/PET/IELTS/TOEFL/PTE
科目 all

Most pop music is influenced, to a greater or lesser degree, by the blues.

多数流行音乐都不同程度地受到了布鲁斯音乐的影响。

delete

删除（文字），擦去（字迹）

vt. [dɪˈliːt]

考试 KET/PET/IELTS/TOEFL/PTE
科目 all

Microblog is required to delete questionable posts.

微博有义务删除有问题的帖子。

deliberate

故意的；从容的；仔细考虑的

adj. [dɪˈlɪbərət]

考试 TOEFL/IELTS/PTE
科目 listening

She spoke in a slow and deliberate way.

她说话慢条斯理不慌不忙。

delicate

易碎的；易生病的，娇弱的；精巧的；微妙的

adj. [ˈdelɪkət]

考试 TOEFL/IELTS/PTE
科目 listening

The eye is one of the most delicate organs of the body.
眼睛是人体最娇贵的器官之一。

D

deliver

投递；解救；发表；接生；交出

v. [dɪˈlɪvə(r)]

考试 KET/PET/IELTS/TOEFL/ PTE
科目 all

She is due to deliver a lecture on genetic engineering.
她根据安排要做一次关于遗传工程的演讲。

delivery

递送；交付；分娩；交货；引渡

n. [dɪˈlɪvəri]

考试 KET/PET/IELTS/TOEFL/ PTE
科目 all

Please pay for goods on delivery.
请货到付款。

demolish

拆毁；废除；驳倒

vt. [dɪˈmɒlɪʃ]

考试 TOEFL/IELTS/PTE
科目 listening

A recent book has demolished this theory.
最近出版的一本书推翻了这种理论。

demonstrate

论证，证明，说明；示威；表达，表现；演示，示范

v. [ˈdemənstreɪt]

考试 TOEFL/IELTS/PTE
科目 reading

Let me demonstrate to you some of the difficulties we are facing.
我来向你们说明一下我们面临的一些困难。

dense

浓密的；密集的；愚笨的

adj. ［dens］

考试 TOEFL/IELTS/PTE
科目 listening

A dense column of smoke rose several miles into the air.
一股浓烟升到了几英里的高空中。

department

部，局，处，科，部门，系

n. ［dɪˈpɑːtmənt］

考试 KET/PET/IELTS/TOEFL/PTE
科目 all

In colleges and universities, every department has its own professors.
在学院和大学，每个系都有自己的教授。

depend

取决于，依靠；信赖，相信

vi. ［dɪˈpend］

考试 KET/PET/IELTS/TOEFL/PTE
科目 all

The community depends on the shipping industry for its survival.
这个地区依靠航运业维持生活。

depict

描绘；描写

vt. ［dɪˈpɪkt］

考试 TOEFL/IELTS/PTE
科目 listening

The advertisements depict smoking as glamorous and attractive.
这些广告把吸烟描绘得充满刺激和富有吸引力。

deplete

耗尽，用尽

vt. ［dɪˈpliːt］

考试 TOEFL/IELTS/PTE
科目 listening

When you deplete your energy, you reduce your ability to focus and accomplish the tasks in your life effectively.
当你大量消耗能量时，你正在削弱自己集中精力并高效完成生活中各项任务的能力。

depress

使沮丧；使萧条；压下；降低

vt. ［dɪˈpres］

考试 TOEFL/IELTS/PTE
科目 listening

There is some psychological evidence that Monday mornings depress us.

一些心理学证据显示，周一的早晨会使我们心情抑郁。

deprive

剥夺，使丧失

vt. ［dɪˈpraɪv］

考试 TOEFL/IELTS/PTE
科目 reading

The planned highway will deprive children of their playground.

规划中的公路将会侵占孩子们的操场.

derive

取得，得到；追溯…的起源（或来由）

v. ［dɪˈraɪv］

考试 TOEFL/IELTS/PTE
科目 reading

He derived great pleasure from painting.

他从绘画中得到了极大的乐趣。

descend

下降，下来；降临，来临；遗传

v. ［dɪˈsend］

考试 TOEFL/IELTS/PTE
科目 listening

He claims to be descended from a Spanish prince.

他声称是一位西班牙王子的后裔。

describe

描述，形容

vt. ［dɪˈskraɪb］

考试 KET/PET/IELTS/TOEFL/PTE
科目 all

He described the meeting as marking a new stage in the peace process.

他称这次会议标志着和平进程进入了一个新阶段。

desert

沙漠

n. [ˈdezət]

考试 KET/PET/IELTS/TOEFL/PTE
科目 all

The vehicles have been modified to suit conditions in the desert.
车辆经过改装以适应沙漠的环境。

deserve

应得，应受

vt. [dɪˈzɜːv]

考试 TOEFL/IELTS/PTE
科目 reading

You deserve a rest after all that hard work.
辛苦劳累那么久，你该休息了。

design

设计；构思；绘制；计划；企图

vt. [dɪˈzaɪn]

考试 KET/PET/IELTS/TOEFL/PTE
科目 all

We are able to design a course to suit your particular needs.
我们可以专门设计一门课程以满足你的特殊需求。

designate

把…定名为，指派，标出

vt. [ˈdezɪɡneɪt]

考试 TOEFL/IELTS/PTE
科目 listening

This floor has been designated a non-smoking area.
这层楼已定为无烟区。

desirable

值得拥有的，吸引人的

adj. [dɪˈzaɪərəbl]

考试 TOEFL/IELTS/PTE
科目 listening

The crowd moved indoors for what were deemed the most desirable items.
人群为了被视为最值得拥有的物品涌入屋里。

dessert

正餐后的水果或甜食

n. ［dɪˈzɜːt］

考试 KET/PET/IELTS/TOEFL/
PTE
科目 all

She had homemade ice cream for dessert.
她用自制的冰激凌作为饭后甜点。

D

destroy

破坏，摧毁，消灭

vt. ［dɪˈstrɔɪ］

考试 KET/PET/IELTS/TOEFL/
PTE
科目 all

No one was injured in the explosion, but the building was completely destroyed.
没有人在爆炸中受伤，但大楼遭到了彻底的毁坏。

detail

细节，详情

n. ［ˈdiːteɪl］

考试 KET/PET/IELTS/TOEFL/
PTE
科目 all

The details of the plan are still being worked out.
这项计划的细节仍在制订中。

detect

发现，发觉；侦察出

vt. ［dɪˈtekt］

考试 TOEFL/IELTS/PTE
科目 listening

Most skin cancers can be cured if detected and treated early.
如果早发现早治疗，大多数皮肤癌是可以治愈的。

deteriorate

恶化，败坏

vi. ［dɪˈtɪəriəreɪt］

考试 TOEFL/IELTS
科目 writing

The discussion quickly deteriorated into an angry argument.
这场讨论迅速演变为愤怒的争吵。

detriment

损害

n. ['detrɪmənt]

考试 TOEFL/IELTS/PTE
科目 reading

Children spend too much time on schoolwork, to the detriment of other activities.

孩子们把太多的时间用于做作业，影响了他们参加其他活动。

develop

发展，开发，研制；加强，增强；显现，显影；发育，生长

v. [dɪ'veləp]

考试 KET/PET/IELTS/TOEFL/PTE
科目 all

It's hard to say at this stage how the market will develop.

在现阶段，很难说市场将会如何发展。

devise

设计，想出

vt. [dɪ'vaɪz]

考试 TOEFL/IELTS/PTE
科目 listening

A new system has been devised to control traffic in the city.

控制城市交通的新系统已经设计出来了。

devote

把……奉献给

vt. [dɪ'vəut]

考试 TOEFL/IELTS/PTE
科目 reading

He decided to devote the rest of his life to scientific investigation.

他决定将自己的余生献给科学研究事业。

diary

日记；日记簿

n. ['daɪəri]

考试 KET/PET/IELTS/TOEFL/PTE
科目 all

The writer's letters and diaries will be published next year.

这位作家的信件和日记将于明年发表。

dictate

听写；口授；命令，支配

v. [dɪkˈteɪt]

考试 TOEFL/IELTS
科目 writing

Everything he dictated was signed and sent out the same day.

他口授的所有内容都签上名并在同一天寄出了。

diet

饮食；规定的饮食；节食

n. [ˈdaɪət]

考试 KET/PET/IELTS/TOEFL/PTE
科目 all

It's never too late to improve your diet.

什么时候改善饮食都为时不晚。

节食；进行规定饮食

vi. [ˈdaɪət]

考试 KET/PET/IELTS/TOEFL/PTE
科目 all

Most of us have dieted at some time in our lives.

我们大多数人都曾在人生的某个时期节食过。

difference

差别，差异，分歧

n. [ˈdɪfrəns]

考试 KET/PET/IELTS/TOEFL/PTE
科目 all

A few kind words at the right time make all the difference.

在适当的时候说几句贴心话效果迥然不同。

dig

挖，掘

v. [dɪg]

考试 KET/PET/IELTS/TOEFL/PTE
科目 all

They are digging up the football field to lay a new surface.

他们正在把足球场挖开铺一层新地面。

diminish

减小，减少，缩小

v. ［dɪˈmɪnɪʃ］

考试 TOEFL/IELTS/PTE
科目 listening

Universities are facing grave problems because of diminishing resources.

由于资源的减少，大学正面临着严峻的问题。

dine

吃饭，进餐

vi. ［daɪn］

考试 TOEFL/IELTS
科目 writing

He dines alone most nights.

大多数晚上他都是一个人用餐。

diplomacy

外交

n. ［dɪˈpləʊməsi］

考试 TOEFL/IELTS/PTE
科目 listening

The talks have now gone into a stage of quiet diplomacy.

会谈现在已经进入了"温和外交"阶段。

direct

径直的

adj. ［dəˈrekt］

考试 KET/PET/IELTS/TOEFL/PTE
科目 all

They'd come on a direct flight from Athens.

他们是搭乘从雅典直飞这里的航班过来的。

径直（地）

adv. ［dəˈrekt］

考试 KET/PET/IELTS/TOEFL/PTE
科目 all

You can fly direct to Amsterdam from most British airports.

从英国的大多数机场都可以直飞阿姆斯特丹。

管理，指导；指向；导演，指挥

v. ［dəˈrekt］

考试 KET/PET/IELTS/TOEFL/
PTE
科目 all

A new manager has been appointed to direct the project.

已任命一位新经理来管理这项工程。

D

direction

方向，方位；指令，说明

n. ［dəˈrekʃn］

考试 KET/PET/IELTS/TOEFL/
PTE
科目 all

The exhibition provides evidence of several new directions in her works.

这次展览表明她的创作有几个新动向。

directly

直接地，径直地；马上，立即

adv. ［dəˈrektli］

考试 KET/PET/IELTS/TOEFL/
PTE
科目 all

He drove her directly to the hotel.

他驾车直接把她送到了旅馆。

director

指导者；主任；导演

n. ［dəˈrektə(r)］

考试 KET/PET/IELTS/TOEFL/
PTE
科目 all

He has been director of the project since its inception.

这项工作从一开始他就是负责人。

disadvantage

不利，不利地位

n. ［ˌdɪsədˈvɑːntɪdʒ］

考试 KET/PET/IELTS/TOEFL/
PTE
科目 all

One major disadvantage of the area is the lack of public transport.

这个地区的一大不便之处就是缺少公共交通工具。

disagree

有分歧；不一致

vi. ［ˌdɪsəˈɡriː］

考试 KET/PET/IELTS/TOEFL/
PTE
科目 all

They can communicate even when they strongly disagree.
即使在有很大分歧时，他们也还是能够交流。

disagreement

不一致；争论

n. ［ˌdɪsəˈɡriːmənt］

考试 KET/PET/IELTS/TOEFL/
PTE
科目 all

Britain and France have expressed some disagreement with the proposal.
英国和法国已经对这项提案发表了一些反对意见。

disallow

不允许；不接受；驳回

vt. ［ˌdɪsəˈlaʊ］

考试 TOEFL/IELTS
科目 writing

The court has announced the award to disallow the claim.
仲裁庭已宣布裁决，驳回上诉。

disappear

不复存在，消失；灭绝，消亡

vi. ［ˌdɪsəˈpɪə(r)］

考试 KET/PET/IELTS/TOEFL/
PTE
科目 all

Our countryside is disappearing at an alarming rate.
我们的农村地区正在以惊人的速度消亡。

disappoint

失望；（希望等）破灭；挫败（计划等）

vt. ［ˌdɪsəˈpɔɪnt］

考试 KET/PET/IELTS/TOEFL/
PTE
科目 all

Her decision to cancel the concert is bound to disappoint her fans.
她决定取消这场音乐会，这肯定会使她的歌迷失望。

disappointed

失望的，扫兴的

adj. [ˌdɪsəˈpɔɪntɪd]

考试 KET/PET/IELTS/TOEFL/PTE
科目 all

I was disappointed to see the lack of coverage afforded to this event.

令我失望的是，这一事件并未得到什么报道。

disastrous

灾难性的；极糟糕的

adj. [dɪˈzɑːstrəs]

考试 TOEFL/IELTS/PTE
科目 listening

Carelessness in driving often results in disastrous accidents.

驾驶不慎常带来灾难性的意外。

discard

抛弃，遗弃

vt. [dɪsˈkɑːd]

考试 TOEFL/IELTS/PTE
科目 listening

Read the manufacturer's guidelines before discarding the box.

在丢掉盒子前先看一下制造商的使用说明。

discipline

训练；纪律；戒律，惩罚；学科

n. [ˈdɪsəplɪn]

考试 TOEFL/IELTS/PTE
科目 reading

He has stressed discipline and control.

他强调了纪律和管控。

discount

折扣

n. [ˈdɪskaʊnt]

考试 KET/PET/IELTS/TOEFL/PTE
科目 all

Full-time staff get a 20 percent discount.

全职员工享受20%的折扣。

D

discuss

讨论，商议

vt. ［dɪˈskʌs］

考试 KET/PET/IELTS/TOEFL/ PTE
科目 all

I will be discussing the situation with colleagues to-morrow.

明天我会和同事们讨论一下情况。

discussion

讨论，谈论；论述

n. ［dɪˈskʌʃn］

考试 KET/PET/IELTS/TOEFL/ PTE
科目 all

The whole question of the school curriculum is up for discussion.

涉及学校课程的全部事项都已提出供大家讨论。

disease

疾病

n. ［dɪˈziːz］

考试 KET/PET/IELTS/TOEFL/ PTE
科目 all

Doctors believe they have cured him of the disease.

医生们相信他们已经治好了他的病。

dish

碟子，盘子；菜肴

n. ［dɪʃ］

考试 KET/PET/IELTS/TOEFL/ PTE
科目 all

Pile potatoes into a warm serving dish.

把土豆倒在一个保温的餐盘。

dismay

灰心，丧气；惊愕

n. ［dɪsˈmeɪ］

考试 TOEFL/IELTS/PTE
科目 listening

To her dismay, her name was not on the list.

使她难过的是，名单上没有她的名字。

dispatch

派遣，发送；迅速办理

vt. [dɪ'spætʃ]

考试 TOEFL/IELTS
科目 writing

Goods are dispatched within 24 hours of your order reaching us.

订单到达我方 24 小时内发货。

D

dispel

驱散；消除（尤指感觉或信仰）

vt. [dɪ'spel]

考试 TOEFL/IELTS
科目 writing

He must dispel this dangerous sense of drift.

他必须消除这种趋势带来的危险感觉。

disperse

使散开，使疏散，使分散

v. [dɪ'spɜːs]

考试 TOEFL/IELTS
科目 writing

The oil appeared to be dispersing.

油好像在扩散。

display

展览，陈列

vt. [dɪ'spleɪ]

考试 KET/PET/IELTS/TOEFL/
PTE
科目 all

The cabinets display seventeenth-century blue-and-white porcelain.

展柜中陈列着 17 世纪的青花瓷。

展览，陈列

n. [dɪ'spleɪ]

考试 KET/PET/IELTS/TOEFL/
PTE
科目 all

Designs for the new sports hall are on display in the library.

新体育馆的设计图展示在图书馆里。

dispute

争论，争执；质疑

v. [dɪˈspjuːt]

考试 TOEFL/IELTS/PTE
科目 reading

The ownership of the land has been disputed for centuries.

这片土地的所有权问题已经争论了几个世纪。

dissipate

消散，消失；浪费，挥霍

v. [ˈdɪsɪpeɪt]

考试 TOEFL/IELTS
科目 writing

The tension in the room had dissipated.

房间里的紧张气氛消失了。

dissolve

使液化，融化；使（固体）溶解；使解散，解除

v. [dɪˈzɒlv]

考试 TOEFL/IELTS/PTE
科目 listening

Heat gently until the sugar dissolves.

慢慢加热直到糖溶解为止。

distinct

清楚的；不同的，独特的

adj. [dɪˈstɪŋkt]

考试 TOEFL/IELTS/PTE
科目 listening

This book is divided into two distinct parts.

这本书分为截然不同的两个部分。

distinguish

区别，识别；成为……的特征；使有别于使显赫

v. [dɪˈstɪŋgwɪʃ]

考试 TOEFL/IELTS/PTE
科目 reading

The male bird is distinguished from the female by its red beak.

雄鸟喙呈红色，有别于雌鸟。

dive

潜水；跳水；俯冲

vi. ［daɪv］

考试 KET/PET/IELTS/TOEFL/
PTE
科目 all

She was standing by a pool，about to dive in.
她当时站在水池旁边，正要往里跳。

潜水；跳水；俯冲

n. ［daɪv］

考试 KET/PET/IELTS/TOEFL/
PTE
科目 all

He is considering a seventh dive next year.
他正在考虑明年的第七次潜水行动。

diver

潜水员；跳水运动员

n. ［ˈdaɪvə(r)］

考试 KET/PET/IELTS/TOEFL/
PTE
科目 all

Two divers work together while a standby diver re-
mains on the surface.
两名潜水员协同工作，同时有一名候补潜水员留在水
面上。

diverse

多种多样的，各不相同的

adj. ［daɪˈvɜːs］

考试 TOEFL/IELTS/PTE
科目 listening

Society is now much more diverse than ever before.
当今社会较之以往任何时候都要丰富多彩得多。

divert

使转向；转移……的注意力；娱乐，供消遣

vt. ［daɪˈvɜːt］

考试 TOEFL/IELTS/PTE
科目 listening

During the strike，ambulances will be diverted to
private hospitals.
在罢工期间，救护车将被转到私人医院。

D

divide

分，划分，分开；分配；除以，除

v.　[dɪˈvaɪd]

考试 KET/PET/IELTS/TOEFL/PTE
科目 all

Divide the pastry in half and roll out each piece.

把面团一分为二，把每块都擀平。

doctor

医生；博士

n.　[ˈdɒktə(r)]

考试 KET/PET/IELTS/TOEFL/PTE
科目 all

He is a Doctor of Philosophy.

他是一名哲学博士。

授予博士学位；诊断；篡改，伪造

vt.　[ˈdɒktə(r)]

考试 KET/PET/IELTS/TOEFL/PTE
科目 all

They doctored the prints to make her look as awful as possible.

他们修改了照片，尽可能地丑化她的容貌。

document

公文，文献

n.　[ˈdɒkjumənt]

考试 KET/PET/IELTS/TOEFL/PTE
科目 all

The foreign ministers of the two countries signed the documents today.

两国的外交大臣今天签署了文件。

documentary

文献的，书面的；纪录的，纪实的

adj.　[ˌdɒkjuˈmentri]

考试 KET/PET/IELTS/TOEFL/PTE
科目 all

The film was given a documentary style by the director.

导演以纪实的表现手法拍摄了这部影片。

纪录片

n. [ˌdɒkjuˈmentri]

考试 TOEFL/IELTS/PTE
科目 listening

The documentary premiered at the Jerusalem Film Festival.

这部纪录片在耶路撒冷电影节首映。

D

dominant

支配的，统治的，占优势的

adj. [ˈdɒmɪnənt]

考试 TOEFL/IELTS/PTE
科目 listening

She was a dominant figure in the French film industry.

她在法国电影界是个举足轻重的人物。

donation

捐赠；捐赠物

n. [dəʊˈneɪʃn]

考试 TOEFL/IELTS/PTE
科目 reading

Employees make regular donations to charity.

员工定期向慈善机构捐赠。

double

成对地；双双地

adv. [ˈdʌbl]

考试 KET/PET/IELTS/TOEFL/
PTE
科目 all

I had to bend double to get under the table.

我必须弓着身子才能钻到桌子底下。

两倍的，双重的

adj. [ˈdʌbl]

考试 KET/PET/IELTS/TOEFL/
PTE
科目 all

The supermarket has the double advantage of being both easy and cheap.

这家超市具有既方便又便宜的双重优点。

使加倍，加倍；把……对折，折叠

v. [ˈdʌbl]

考试 KET/PET/IELTS/TOEFL/PTE
科目 all

Her baby doubled its weight in a year.

她的婴儿在一年内体重增加了一倍。

Membership almost doubled in two years.

两年内会员人数几乎翻了一倍。

doubt

怀疑，疑虑

n. [daʊt]

考试 KET/PET/IELTS/TOEFL/PTE
科目 all

The article raised doubts about how effective the new drug really was.

这篇文章对这种新药的实效有多大提出了疑问。

怀疑，疑虑

vt. [daʊt]

考试 KET/PET/IELTS/TOEFL/PTE
科目 all

No one doubted his ability.

没有人怀疑他的能力。

dove

鸽子

n. [dʌv]

考试 KET/PET/IELTS/TOEFL/PTE
科目 all

Noah lets a dove fly out of the ship.

诺亚让一只鸽子飞出了船舱。

downstairs

在楼下，往楼下

adv. [ˌdaʊnˈsteəz]

考试 KET/PET/IELTS/TOEFL/PTE
科目 all

Everybody was downstairs watching a movie.

大家都在楼下看电影。

dozen

一打，十二个

n. [ˈdʌzn]

考试 KET/PET/IELTS/TOEFL/
PTE
科目 all

He ordered a dozen of red roses.

他订购了 12 朵红玫瑰。

draft

草稿；汇票；征兵

n. [drɑːft]

考试 KET/PET/IELTS/TOEFL/
PTE
科目 all

I faxed a first draft of this article to him.

我将这篇文章的初稿传真给他了。

drama

剧本，戏剧；戏剧性事件或场面

n. [ˈdrɑːmə]

考试 KET/PET/IELTS/TOEFL/
PTE
科目 all

A powerful human drama was unfolding before our eyes.

一个极富人情味的戏剧性事件在我们的眼前上演了。

dramatize

使戏剧化，夸张

v. [ˈdræmətaɪz]

考试 TOEFL/IELTS
科目 writing

They have a tendency to show off，to dramatize almost every situation.

他们爱炫耀，几乎会夸大各种情况。

draw

拉；画；抽出；吸引；挨近

v. [drɔː]

考试 KET/PET/IELTS/TOEFL/
PTE
科目 all

She would sit there drawing with the pencil stub.

她会坐在那儿用铅笔头画画。

drawback

缺点；障碍；不利条件

n. [ˈdrɔːbæk]

考试 TOEFL/IELTS/PTE
科目 listening

He felt the apartment's only drawback was that it was too small.
他觉得这间公寓的唯一缺点就是太小了。

drawing

绘图，图样；素描画

n. [ˈdrɔːɪŋ]

考试 KET/PET/IELTS/TOEFL/PTE
科目 all

She did a drawing of me.
她为我画了张素描。

drop

下降，减少；滴；落下；微量

n. [drɒp]

考试 KET/PET/IELTS/TOEFL/PTE
科目 all

The poll indicates a drop in support for the Conservatives.
民意测验表明保守党的支持率有所下降。

落下；下降

v. [drɒp]

考试 KET/PET/IELTS/TOEFL/PTE
科目 all

Temperatures can drop to freezing at night.
夜间温度可能会降到零度以下。

drought

干旱

n. [draʊt]

考试 TOEFL/IELTS/PTE
科目 listening

The drought is not bad news for every farmer.
干旱并非对所有农民都是坏消息。

drug

药物；毒品

n. [drʌg]

考试 KET/PET/IELTS/TOEFL/ PTE
科目 all

The doctor put me on a course of pain-killing drugs.
医生让我服一个疗程的止痛药。

下麻醉药；用药麻醉；使服兴奋剂

v. [drʌg]

考试 KET/PET/IELTS/TOEFL/ PTE
科目 all

It's illegal to drug horses before a race.
赛前给马服用兴奋剂是违法的。

drum

鼓；鼓状物；鼓声

n. [drʌm]

考试 KET/PET/IELTS/TOEFL/ PTE
科目 all

At dusk, a huge drum begins to beat.
黄昏时分，一只巨大的鼓开始敲击。

drunk

醉酒的；陶醉的

adj. [drʌŋk]

考试 KET/PET/IELTS/TOEFL/ PTE
科目 all

His only way of dealing with his problems was to go out and get drunk.
他解决烦心事的唯一办法就是出去喝个烂醉。

酗酒者，醉汉

n. [drʌŋk]

考试 KET/PET/IELTS/TOEFL/ PTE
科目 all

A drunk lay in the alley.
一个酒鬼躺在小胡同里。

D

dry

干（旱）的；干渴的；枯燥的

adj. ［draɪ］

考试 KET/PET/IELTS/TOEFL/
PTE
科目 all

The wells in most villages in the region have run dry.

这个地区多数村庄的水井都已干涸。

（使）变干，晒干

v. ［draɪ］

考试 KET/PET/IELTS/TOEFL/
PTE
科目 all

Hot sun and cold winds can soon dry out your skin.

火辣辣的太阳和寒风可使你的皮肤很快变干燥。

dull

阴暗的；迟钝的；沉闷的；钝的

adj. ［dʌl］

考试 KET/PET/IELTS/TOEFL/
PTE
科目 all

He thought the countryside was flat, dull and uninteresting.

他当时认为农村地区缺乏生气，无聊乏味。

减轻；使迟钝；使不活泼，（使）变得无光泽

v. ［dʌl］

考试 KET/PET/IELTS/TOEFL/
PTE
科目 all

Her eyes dulled and she gazed blankly.

她双目变得黯然无神，茫然凝神。

dust

灰尘，尘土

n. ［dʌst］

考试 KET/PET/IELTS/TOEFL/
PTE
科目 all

He reversed into the stockade in a cloud of dust.

他在一阵尘土中将车倒进了围栏。

拂去，掸去；擦去

v. [dʌst]

考试 KET/PET/IELTS/TOEFL/
PTE
科目 all

She dusted some ash from her sleeve.
她掸去袖子上的灰尘。

duty

义务，责任；职务；税

n. ['djuːti]

考试 KET/PET/IELTS/TOEFL/
PTE
科目 all

My duty is to look after the animals.
我的责任就是照看这些动物。

duty-free

免税的

adj. [ˌdjuːti'friː]

考试 KET/PET/IELTS/TOEFL/
PTE
科目 all

The Chinese have become the world's biggest duty-free shoppers.
中国人已成为世界上最大的免税消费者。

dwell

居住；详述

vi. [dwel]

考试 TOEFL/IELTS/PTE
科目 reading

They are concerned for the fate of the forest and the Indians who dwell in it.
他们为这片森林及居住于其中的印第安人的命运而担心。

dynamic

动态的；精力充沛的；力的，动力的

adj. [daɪ'næmɪk]

考试 TOEFL/IELTS/PTE
科目 listening

He seemed a dynamic and energetic leader.
他似乎是一位富有干劲、精力充沛的领导。

D

E

earn

赚得，挣得；获得

v. ［ɜːn］

KET/PET/IELTS/TOEFL/PTE
科目 all

As a teacher, she had earned the respect and admiration of her students.

作为教师，她得到了学生们的尊敬和钦佩。

earthquake

地震

n. ［ˈɜːθkweɪk］

考试 KET/PET/IELTS/TOEFL/PTE
科目 all

Devastating earthquake is generally shallow earthquake.

破坏性地震一般是浅源地震。

Easter

复活节

n. ［ˈiːstə(r)］

考试 KET/PET/IELTS/TOEFL/PTE
科目 all

The government declared Easter Monday a public holiday.

政府宣布复活节后的星期一是公共假日。

eccentricity

古怪行为，怪僻

n. ［ˌeksenˈtrɪsəti］

考试 TOEFL/IELTS/PTE
科目 listening

We all have our little eccentricities.

我们都有些小的怪癖。

136

eclipse

（日、月）食；丧失，黯然失色；暗淡

n. [ɪˈklɪps]

考试 TOEFL/IELTS/PTE
科目 reading

Her work was in eclipse for most of the 20th century.

她的作品在 20 世纪大部分时间里都湮没无闻。

E

edge

边，棱；刀口，刃

n. [edʒ]

考试 KET/PET/IELTS/TOEFL/ PTE
科目 all

She was standing at the water's edge.

她正站在水边。

侧身移动，挤进

v. [edʒ]

考试 KET/PET/IELTS/TOEFL/ PTE
科目 all

He edged closer to the telephone, ready to grab it.

他慢慢地靠近电话，准备抓起它。

edit

编辑，剪辑

v. [ˈedɪt]

考试 KET/PET/IELTS/TOEFL/ PTE
科目 all

He taught me to edit and splice films.

他教我电影剪接。

effect

结果；效果；影响；印象

n. [ɪˈfekt]

考试 KET/PET/IELTS/TOEFL/ PTE
科目 all

Parents worry about the effect of music on their adolescents' behaviour.

父母担心音乐对青春期孩子的行为所产生的影响。

招致；实现；达到

vt. ［ɪˈfekt］

考试 KET/PET/IELTS/TOEFL/
PTE
科目 all

Prospects for effecting real political change seemed
to have taken a major step backwards.
实现真正政治变革的机会似乎变得更加渺茫了。

effective

有效的，生效的；被实施的

adj. ［ɪˈfektɪv］

考试 TOEFL/IELTS/PTE
科目 reading

Effective communication needs time management.
有效沟通需要统筹时间。

efficiency

效率；功效

n. ［ɪˈfɪʃnsi］

考试 TOEFL/IELTS/PTE
科目 reading

How are you managing the workload when
efficiency isn't enough?
当你工作效率不高的时候，你是怎样调整你的工作量
的呢?

effort

努力；成就；艰难的尝试

n. ［ˈefət］

考试 TOEFL/IELTS/PTE
科目 listening

Finding a cure requires considerable time and
effort.
找到治疗的办法需要大量的时间和精力。

Egypt

埃及

n. ［ˈiːdʒɪpt］

考试 TOEFL/IELTS/PTE
科目 listening

Egypt has a large domestic consumer market.
埃及拥有广阔的国内消费市场。

Egyptian

埃及的

adj. [ɪˈdʒɪpʃn]

考试 TOEFL/IELTS/PTE
科目 listening

The ancient Egyptian civilization is one of the oldest in the world.

古埃及文化是世界上最古老的文化之一。

E

埃及人

n. [ɪˈdʒɪpʃn]

考试 TOEFL/IELTS/PTE
科目 listening

Many things left by the ancient Egyptians in tombs have been brought to light.

在古埃及的古陵墓中发掘出了很多东西。

elaborate

精心计划的；复杂的，详尽的

adj. [ɪˈlæbərət]

考试 TOEFL/IELTS/PTE
科目 listening

The whole thing was an elaborate prank!

整件事就是一个精心设计的恶作剧！

electric

电的，导电的，电动的

adj. [ɪˈlektrɪk]

考试 KET/PET/IELTS/TOEFL/PTE
科目 all

Electric cars are evolving quickly.

电动汽车的发展日新月异。

electrical

电的，电气科学的

adj. [ɪˈlektrɪkl]

考试 KET/PET/IELTS/TOEFL/PTE
科目 all

The aircraft made an unscheduled landing after developing an electrical fault.

飞机由于发生电力故障而临时降落。

electricity

电，电能；电学

n. ［ɪˌlekˈtrɪsəti］

考试 KET/PET/IELTS/TOEFL/PTE
科目 all

The electricity had been cut off.
停电了。

elementary

基本的，初级的

adj. ［ˌelɪˈmentri］

考试 KET/PET/IELTS/TOEFL/PTE
科目 all

Elementary education should be available to all children.
所有的儿童都应当接受初等教育。

elevate

提升……的职位；改善；使情绪高昂；举起，使上升

vt. ［ˈelɪveɪt］

考试 TOEFL/IELTS/PTE
科目 listening

Smoking often elevates blood pressure.
抽烟常常使血压升高。

elevator

电梯，升降机

n. ［ˈelɪveɪtə(r)］

考试 KET/PET/IELTS/TOEFL/PTE
科目 all

The elevator broke down and we had to walk up the tenth floor.
电梯坏了，我们只好走到十层。

eliminate

排除，清除；消灭；淘汰

vt. ［ɪˈlɪmɪneɪt］

考试 TOEFL/IELTS/PTE
科目 listening

If you think you may be allergic to a food or drink, eliminate it from your diet.
如果你觉得自己可能对某种食物或饮料过敏，就将其从日常饮食中除去。

elimination

消灭，排除，消除

n. [ɪˌlɪmɪˈneɪʃn]

TOEFL/IELTS/PTE
reading

There were three eliminations in the first round of the competition.

比赛第一轮淘汰了三个队。

embark

上船；从事；开始

v. [ɪmˈbɑːk]

TOEFL/IELTS
writing

He's embarking on a new career as a writer.

他即将开始新的职业生涯——当一名作家。

embarrass

使为难，使尴尬

vt. [ɪmˈbærəs]

KET/PET/IELTS/TOEFL/PTE
all

It embarrassed him that he had no idea of what was going on.

对所发生的事情一无所知，这让他很难堪。

embassy

大使馆

n. [ˈembəsi]

KET/PET/IELTS/TOEFL/PTE
all

The Russian Embassy has already complained.

俄罗斯大使馆已经提出了抗议。

embody

体现，使具体化；包含，收录

vt. [ɪmˈbɒdi]

TOEFL/IELTS/PTE
listening

The new edition embodies many improvements.

新版本有许多改进之处。

embrace

拥抱；欣然接受；利用；包含

v. [ɪmˈbreɪs]

考试 TOEFL/IELTS/PTE
科目 listening

He threw his arms round her and they embraced passionately.

他伸出手臂搂住她，他们热情相拥。

emission

排放；散发；传播；散发物，排放物

n. [ɪˈmɪʃn]

考试 TOEFL/IELTS/PTE
科目 listening

Most scientists accept that climate change is linked to carbon emissions.

大多数科学家相信气候变化与碳排放量有关。

emphasize

强调，加强……的语气；使突出，使明显

vt. [ˈemfəsaɪz]

考试 TOEFL/IELTS/PTE
科目 reading

Among these reasons for the accident, one should be emphasized that mechanism failure contributed to it dramatically.

在引起事故的众多原因中，应强调的一点是，机械故障极大地促成了这一事故。

employ

雇用；运用，使用

n. [ɪmˈplɔɪ]

考试 KET/PET/IELTS/TOEFL/PTE
科目 all

The agent was in the employ of a foreign organization.

这名特工是一个境外组织雇用的。

雇用；运用，使用

vt. [ɪmˈplɔɪ]

考试 KET/PET/IELTS/TOEFL/PTE
科目 all

A number of people have been employed to deal with the backlog of work.

已雇来一些人处理积压的工作。

empty

空的；空洞的

adj. ['empti]

考试 KET/PET/IELTS/TOEFL/
PTE
科目 all

The room was bare and empty.

房间空荡荡的。

encircle

环绕；包围

vt. [ɪn'sɜːkl]

考试 TOEFL/IELTS
科目 writing

By 22nd November the Sixth Army was encircled.

到 11 月 22 日，第六军被包围了。

encounter

遭遇；意外地遇到

vt. [ɪn'kaʊntə(r)]

考试 TOEFL/IELTS/PTE
科目 reading

Did you encounter anyone in the building?

你在大楼里遇到什么人了吗？

encourage

鼓励；怂恿

vt. [ɪn'kʌrɪdʒ]

考试 KET/PET/IELTS/TOEFL/
PTE
科目 all

We want to encourage people to go fishing, not put them off.

我们希望鼓励人们去垂钓，而不是打消他们的热情。

endeavour

努力，尽力，力图

v. [ɪn'devə(r)]

考试 TOEFL/IELTS/PTE
科目 reading

The sick man did not endeavour to get better.

那个病人没有努力使自己的病情好一点。

endorse

签署（姓名）；赞同

vt. ［ɪnˈdɔːs］

考试 TOEFL/IELTS/PTE
科目 listening

I can endorse their opinion wholeheartedly.
我可以全力支持他们的意见。

endurance

忍耐力，耐久力

n. ［ɪnˈdjʊərəns］

考试 TOEFL/IELTS/PTE
科目 reading

The exercise obviously will improve strength and endurance.
这种锻炼会明显改善体力，增加耐力。

endure

忍受；持久，持续

v. ［ɪnˈdjʊə(r)］

考试 TOEFL/IELTS
科目 writing

Somehow the language endures and continues to survive.
那种语言以某种方式保存了下来，并继续存在下去。

energetic

精力旺盛的，精力充沛的

adj. ［ˌenəˈdʒetɪk］

考试 TOEFL/IELTS/PTE
科目 reading

Ten-year-olds are incredibly energetic.
10岁的孩子精力格外旺盛。

energy

活力，精力；能，能量

n. ［ˈenədʒi］

考试 KET/PET/IELTS/TOEFL/PTE
科目 all

At 54 years old her energy and looks are magnificent.
她54岁了，精力和气色都非常好。

engineer

工程师

n. ［ˌendʒɪˈnɪə(r)］

考试 KET/PET/IELTS/TOEFL/ PTE
科目 all

I am a software engineer and a tech entrepreneur.

我是一名软件工程师和科技企业家。

enhance

提高（强度、力量、数量等）；增强（进）

vt. ［ɪnˈhɑːns］

考试 TOEFL/IELTS/PTE
科目 listening

This is an opportunity to enhance the reputation of the company.

这是提高公司声誉的机会。

enlighten

启发，开导

vt. ［ɪnˈlaɪtn］

考试 TOEFL/IELTS/PTE
科目 reading

If you know what is wrong with her, please enlighten me.

如果你知道她出什么问题了，请告诉我。

enormous

庞大的，巨大的

adj. ［ɪˈnɔːməs］

考试 TOEFL/IELTS/PTE
科目 reading

The main bedroom is enormous.

这间主卧非常大。

enquire

询问，打听

v. ［ɪnˈkwaɪə(r)］

考试 TOEFL/IELTS
科目 writing

She rang up to enquire when her car would be ready.

她打电话询问她的车什么时候能准备好。

E

enrich

使丰富，充实；使富有

vt. ［ɪnˈrɪtʃ］

考试 TOEFL/IELTS/PTE
科目 reading

An extended family enriches life in many ways.

大家庭在很多方面会使生活更加丰富多彩。

enter

进入；参加，加入；写入

v. ［ˈentə(r)］

考试 KET/PET/IELTS/TOEFL/PTE
科目 all

He entered the firm as a junior associate.

他作为一名初级职员进入了该公司。

Only four British players have entered for the championship.

只有四名英国运动员报名参加锦标赛。

enthusiasm

热情，热心；狂热；积极性

n. ［ɪnˈθjuːziæzəm］

考试 TOEFL/IELTS/PTE
科目 reading

How do you rediscover the enthusiasm of your childhood?

你又是如何重新看待自己童年时期的热情呢？

entrust

委托，托付

vt. ［ɪnˈtrʌst］

考试 TOEFL/IELTS
科目 writing

Can you entrust an assistant with the task?

你能把这项工作交给助手吗？

envelop

包住；围绕

v. ［ɪnˈveləp］

考试 TOEFL/IELTS
科目 writing

That lovely, rich fragrant smell of the forest enveloped us.

森林里那种馥郁芬芳的迷人气味围绕着我们。

envelope

信封；塑料封皮；封套

n. [ˈenvələʊp]

考试 KET/PET/IELTS/TOEFL/PTE
科目 all

The envelope could contain every secret she's ever had.

那个信封里可能包含了她所有的秘密。

environment

环境；生态环境，自然环境

n. [ɪnˈvaɪrənmənt]

考试 KET/PET/IELTS/TOEFL/PTE
科目 all

Pupils in our schools are taught in a safe, secure environment.

我们学校的学生在安全无虞的环境中接受教育。

equipment

设备，器材，装置；才能

n. [ɪˈkwɪpmənt]

考试 KET/PET/IELTS/TOEFL/PTE
科目 all

Sales of construction equipment have plummeted.

建筑设备的销售大幅下滑。

eradicate

根除

vt. [ɪˈrædɪkeɪt]

考试 TOEFL/IELTS
科目 writing

If tedious tasks could be eradicated, the world would be a much better place.

如果可以消灭那些单调乏味的工作，世界将会变得更加美好。

erect

建立，竖立

vt. [ɪˈrekt]

考试 TOEFL/IELTS/PTE
科目 listening

Police had to erect barriers to keep crowds back.

警察只好设立路障来阻截人群。

error

錯誤，过失

n. [ˈerə(r)]

考试 KET/PET/IELTS/TOEFL/PTE
科目 all

No payments were made last week because of a computer error.

由于计算机出错，上周未支付任何款项。

escalator

电动扶梯

n. [ˈeskəleɪtə(r)]

考试 KET/PET/IELTS/TOEFL/PTE
科目 all

Take the escalator over there and turn right; you'll see the sign.

到那边乘坐自动扶梯，然后往右拐，您就会看到指示牌。

escape

逃跑，逃脱

n. [ɪˈskeɪp]

考试 KET/PET/IELTS/TOEFL/PTE
科目 all

For her travel was an escape from the boredom of her everyday life.

对她来说，旅行是为了从乏味的日常生活中解脱出来。

逃跑；避开，避免

v. [ɪˈskeɪp]

考试 KET/PET/IELTS/TOEFL/PTE
科目 all

A prisoner has escaped from a jail in northern England.

一名囚犯从英格兰北部的一所监狱中逃跑了。

especially

特别，尤其，格外；专门地，主要地

v. [ɪˈspeʃəli]

考试 KET/PET/IELTS/TOEFL/PTE
科目 all

Millions of wild flowers colour the valleys, especially in April and May.

尤其是在四五月份，不计其数的野花盛开，山谷里一片绚烂的色彩。

essence

本质，实质

n. ['esns]

考试 TOEFL/IELTS/PTE
科目 listening

The essence of globalization must be enforced co-operation.

全球化的本质必然是强制性的合作。

establish

建立；确立；证实；使人接受

vt. [ɪ'stæblɪʃ]

考试 KET/PET/IELTS/TOEFL/PTE
科目 all

The School was established in 1989 by an Italian professor.

这所学院是一位意大利教授于 1989 年创建的。

Europe

欧洲

n. ['juərəp]

考试 KET/PET/IELTS/TOEFL/PTE
科目 all

The Channel Tunnel project is the biggest civil engineering project in Europe.

英吉利海峡隧道是欧洲最大的土木工程。

European

欧洲的

adj. [ˌjuərə'piːən]

考试 KET/PET/IELTS/TOEFL/PTE
科目 all

Structural unemployment is surely inching closer to European levels.

结构性失业肯定会缓慢逼近欧洲的水平。

欧洲人

n. [ˌjuərə'piːən]

考试 KET/PET/IELTS/TOEFL/PTE
科目 all

Three quarters of working-age Americans work, compared with roughly 60% of Europeans.

3/4 处于工作年龄的美国人在工作，相比之下，在工作的欧洲人约为 60%。

evaluate

估……的价，定……的值；估计；评价

vt. [ɪˈvæljueɪt]

考试 TOEFL/IELTS/PTE
科目 reading

The market situation is difficult to evaluate.
市场状况难以评价。

even

一致的；双数的；均等的

adj. [ˈiːvn]

考试 KET/PET/IELTS/TOEFL/PTE
科目 all

Divide the dough into 12 even pieces and shape each piece into a ball.
把面团分为 12 等份，并把每一份面团揉成球形。

（使）相等；（使）平均

v. [ˈiːvn]

考试 KET/PET/IELTS/TOEFL/PTE
科目 all

You have to wait until the water level in the pipes evens out.
你得等一等，直到各根管子中的水位一样高。

即使，甚至

adv. [ˈiːvn]

考试 KET/PET/IELTS/TOEFL/PTE
科目 all

Even dark-skinned women should use sunscreens.
即使黑皮肤的女性也应该涂抹防晒霜。

event

事件，事情，大事

n. [ɪˈvent]

考试 KET/PET/IELTS/TOEFL/PTE
科目 all

In any event, he seems to lack a strategy.
无论处理什么大事，他似乎总是缺乏谋略。

evidence

明显；显著；根据；证据；迹象

n. [ˈevɪdəns]

考试 KET/PET/IELTS/TOEFL/PTE
科目 all

To date there is no evidence to support the theory.

到目前为止，还没有证据支持这种理论。

E

evolve

(使) 发展；(使) 进化；(使) 进展

v. [iˈvɒlv]

考试 TOEFL/IELTS
科目 writing

As medical knowledge evolves , beliefs change.

随着医学知识的逐步发展，观念也在发生变化。

exalt

抬高，赞扬

vt. [ɪgˈzɔːlt]

考试 TOEFL/IELTS
科目 writing

His works exalt all those virtues that we are taught to hold dear.

他的作品颂扬了我们所有人应该珍视的美德。

examination

考试，测验；调查；考查；考察

n. [ɪgˌzæmɪˈneɪʃn]

考试 KET/PET/IELTS/TOEFL/PTE
科目 all

Careful examination of the ruins revealed an even earlier temple.

仔细考察这片废墟后发现了一座更为古老的庙宇。

example

例子，实例；模范，榜样

n. [ɪgˈzɑːmpl]

考试 KET/PET/IELTS/TOEFL/PTE
科目 all

It is important to cite examples to support your argument.

用实例来证明你的论点是很重要的。

exasperate

激怒，使恼火

vt. [ɪɡˈzæspəreɪt]

考试 TOEFL/IELTS
科目 writing

We were exasperated at his ill behaviour.
我们对他的恶劣行为感到非常恼怒。

excellent

卓越的，极好的

adj. [ˈeksələnt]

考试 TOEFL/IELTS/PTE
科目 listening

The recording quality is excellent.
录音质量非常好。

except

除……之外

prep. [ɪkˈsept]

考试 KET/PET/IELTS/TOEFL/
PTE
科目 all

I wouldn't have accepted anything except a job in
Europe.
除了去欧洲工作外，我本来什么都不会接受。

exceptional

优越的，杰出的；特殊的，例外的

adj. [ɪkˈsepʃənl]

考试 TOEFL/IELTS/PTE
科目 listening

His translation is exceptional in its poetic quality.
他的译作非常有诗意。

excess

超越，超过；过度，过分；放肆行为

n. [ɪkˈses]

考试 TOEFL/IELTS/PTE
科目 listening

An excess of house plants in a small flat can be
oppressive.
在小公寓中摆放过多室内植物会让人觉得很压抑。

exchange

交换；兑换

v. [ɪksˈtʃeɪndʒ]

考试 KET/PET/IELTS/TOEFL/
PTE
科目 all

We exchanged addresses and Christmas cards.
我们交换了地址和圣诞贺卡。

交换；兑换

n. [ɪksˈtʃeɪndʒ]

考试 KET/PET/IELTS/TOEFL/
PTE
科目 all

Their first exchange set the tone for a new relationship.
他们初步交换了意见，为建立新关系定下了基调。

excite

刺激，使激动；激发，激励

vt. [ɪkˈsaɪt]

考试 KET/PET/IELTS/TOEFL/
PTE
科目 all

We'd not been excited by anything for about three years.
已经有大约三年的时间没有任何事情令我们激动了。

excited

兴奋的，激动的

adj. [ɪkˈsaɪtɪd]

考试 KET/PET/IELTS/TOEFL/
PTE
科目 all

I was so excited when I went to sign the paperwork that I could hardly write.
去签文件时我非常兴奋，几乎无法写字。

exciting

令人兴奋的，使人激动的

adj. [ɪkˈsaɪtɪŋ]

考试 KET/PET/IELTS/TOEFL/
PTE
科目 all

The race itself is very exciting.
比赛本身非常刺激。

E

exclusive

独占的；排外的；孤高的；唯一的；高级的

adj. [ɪkˈskluːsɪv]

考试 TOEFL/IELTS/PTE
科目 listening

He is already a member of Britain's most exclusive club.

他已经是英国最高级俱乐部的成员了。

excuse

原谅，宽恕；免除

vt. [ɪkˈskjuːz]

考试 KET/PET/IELTS/TOEFL/PTE
科目 all

She is usually excused from her duties during the school holidays.

在学校放假期间，她通常不必担负职责。

借口，辩解

n. [ɪkˈskjuːs]

考试 KET/PET/IELTS/TOEFL/PTE
科目 all

It is easy to find excuses for his indecisiveness.

为他的犹豫不决寻找借口是很容易的。

exercise

练习，习题；训练，锻炼

n. [ˈeksəsaɪz]

考试 KET/PET/IELTS/TOEFL/PTE
科目 all

Lack of exercise can lead to feelings of depression and exhaustion.

缺乏锻炼会导致抑郁和疲劳。

训练，锻炼；行使，使用，运用

v. [ˈeksəsaɪz]

考试 KET/PET/IELTS/TOEFL/PTE
科目 all

She exercises two or three times a week.

她每周锻炼两三次。

exert

发挥，行使；努力

vt. [ɪɡ'zɜːt]

考试 TOEFL/IELTS/PTE
科目 listening

Do not exert yourself unnecessarily.

不要做无谓的努力。

exhibition

展览会；（一批）展览品；陈列，展览；表现，显示

n. [ˌeksɪ'bɪʃn]

考试 KET/PET/IELTS/TOEFL/PTE
科目 all

A new exhibition signals the end of postmodernism.

一场新展览会标志着后现代主义的终结。

exit

出口，通道

n. ['eksɪt]

考试 KET/PET/IELTS/TOEFL/PTE
科目 all

He picked up the case and walked towards the exit.

他提起箱子，向出口走去。

expand

（使）扩大，扩展；膨胀；细谈，详述

v. [ɪk'spænd]

考试 TOEFL/IELTS/PTE
科目 reading

We have to expand the size of the image.

我们不得不放大图像的尺寸。

expect

预期；期望，指望；猜想，认为

v. [ɪk'spekt]

考试 KET/PET/IELTS/TOEFL/PTE
科目 all

The talks are expected to continue until tomorrow.

会谈预计将持续到明天。

expectation

预期，期望，指望

n. [ˌekspekˈteɪʃn]

考试 KET/PET/IELTS/TOEFL/ PTE
科目 all

Some parents have unrealistic expectations of their children.
有些父母对孩子的期望不切实际。

expedite

加快，急送

vt. [ˈekspədaɪt]

考试 TOEFL/IELTS/PTE
科目 listening

We tried to help you expedite your plans.
我们尽力帮你加快实现你的计划。

expensive

花钱多的，昂贵的

adj. [ɪkˈspensɪv]

考试 KET/PET/IELTS/TOEFL/ PTE
科目 all

Wine is very expensive in this country.
葡萄酒在这个国家非常昂贵。

experience

经验；经历；体验；阅历

n. [ɪkˈspɪəriəns]

考试 KET/PET/IELTS/TOEFL/ PTE
科目 all

Moving has become a common experience for me.
搬家对我而言已经成了常事。

经受；经历；体验；感受

vt. [ɪkˈspɪəriəns]

考试 KET/PET/IELTS/TOEFL/ PTE
科目 all

British business is now experiencing a severe recession.
英国商业现在正在经历严重的衰退。

experiment

实验；试验；尝试；实践

n. [ɪkˈsperɪmənt]

考试 KET/PET/IELTS/TOEFL/ PTE
科目 all

This question can be answered only by experiment.
只有实验才能解决这个问题。

进行实验；做试验；尝试；试用

vi. [ɪkˈsperɪmənt]

考试 KET/PET/IELTS/TOEFL/ PTE
科目 all

The scientists have already experimented at each other's test sites.
科学家们已经在彼此的实验场所进行了实验。

expert

专家；能手

n. [ˈekspɜːt]

考试 KET/PET/IELTS/TOEFL/ PTE
科目 all

The cook was an expert at making sauces.
那位厨师是调制味汁的能手。

熟练的，有经验的；专门的

adj. [ˈekspɜːt]

考试 KET/PET/IELTS/TOEFL/ PTE
科目 all

The Japanese are expert at lowering manufacturing costs.
日本人在降低制造成本方面很在行。

expertise

专门知识，专门技能

n. [ˌekspɜːˈtiːz]

考试 TOEFL/IELTS/PTE
科目 reading

The problem is that most local authorities lack the expertise to deal sensibly in this market.
问题是大多数地方政府都缺乏合理应对这个市场的专门知识。

explain

解释，说明

v. [ɪkˈspleɪn]

考试 KET/PET/IELTS/TOEFL/PTE
科目 all

Not every judge, however, has the ability to explain the law in simple terms.

然而，不是每个法官都能用简单的语言来解释法律。

explanation

解释，说明

n. [ˌekspləˈneɪʃn]

考试 KET/PET/IELTS/TOEFL/PTE
科目 all

There was a hint of schoolboy shyness in his explanation.

他的解释中带有一丝学生的羞涩。

exploit

英勇的行为；辉煌的功绩

n. [ˈeksplɔɪt]

考试 TOEFL/IELTS/PTE
科目 listening

His wartime exploits were later made into a film and a television series.

他战时的英勇事迹后来被改编成了电影和电视剧。

expose

使暴露，揭发，使曝光；使面临，使遭受（危险或不快）

vt. [ɪkˈspəʊz]

考试 TOEFL/IELTS/PTE
科目 reading

For an instant his whole back was exposed.

一瞬间，他的整个背部都露出来了。

express

表达，表示

vt. [ɪkˈspres]

考试 KET/PET/IELTS/TOEFL/PTE
科目 all

He expresses himself easily in English.

他轻松地用英语表达了自己的观点。

特快的，快速的

adj. [ɪkˈspres]

考试 KET/PET/IELTS/TOEFL/
PTE
科目 all

A special express service is available by fax.
提供传真特快专递服务。

特快列车，快车，快运

n. [ɪkˈspres]

考试 KET/PET/IELTS/TOEFL/
PTE
科目 all

He had boarded an express for Rome.
他已经登上了前往罗马的特快列车。

exquisite

优美的，精巧的

adj. [ɪkˈskwɪzɪt]

考试 TOEFL/IELTS/PTE
科目 listening

The room was decorated in exquisite taste.
这个房间的装饰情趣高雅。

extend

伸出，延长；给予；扩大；适用于，包括

v. [ɪkˈstend]

考试 TOEFL/IELTS/PTE
科目 listening

The school is extending the range of subjects taught.
学校正在拓宽授课学科的范围。

extensive

广大的，广阔的

adj. [ɪkˈstensɪv]

考试 TOEFL/IELTS/PTE
科目 reading

When built, the palace and its grounds were more extensive than the city itself.
建成时，宫殿及其庭园比城市本身的面积还要大。

extensively

广泛地

adv. [ɪkˈstensɪvli]

考试 TOEFL/IELTS/PTE
科目 reading

All these issues have been extensively researched in recent years.

近年来，对所有这些问题都进行了广泛的研究。

extinct

灭绝的；（火山）不再活跃的；（风俗）废弃的

adj. [ɪkˈstɪŋkt]

考试 TOEFL/IELTS/PTE
科目 listening

It is 250 years since the wolf became extinct in this area.

狼在该地区已经灭绝250年了。

extra

额外的

adj. [ˈekstrə]

考试 KET/PET/IELTS/TOEFL/PTE
科目 all

Extra staff have been taken on to cover busy periods.

额外雇用了一些员工来应付繁忙时期。

额外，另外；非常，特别

adv. [ˈekstrə]

考试 KET/PET/IELTS/TOEFL/PTE
科目 all

You may be charged 10% extra for this service.

这项服务可能需要你额外支付10%的费用。

额外事物；额外的人

n. [ˈekstrə]

考试 KET/PET/IELTS/TOEFL/PTE
科目 all

Optional extras include cooking tuition at a top restaurant.

可选的额外项目包括在顶级餐厅学习厨艺的费用。

F

fabricate

捏造，编造（谎言、借口等）；建造，制造

vt. ['fæbrɪkeɪt]

考试 TOEFL/IELTS
科目 writing

All four claim that officers fabricated evidence against them.
四人都声称警察捏造证据陷害他们。

facilitate

使便利

vt. [fə'sɪlɪteɪt]

考试 TOEFL/IELTS/PTE
科目 listening

The new airport will facilitate the development of tourism.
新机场将促进旅游业的发展。

facility

设备，设施；天资，才能，天赋

n. [fə'sɪləti]

考试 TOEFL/IELTS/PTE
科目 reading

The hotel has special facilities for welcoming disabled people.
这家旅馆有专供残疾人使用的设施。

fact

事实，实际

n. [fækt]

考试 KET/PET/IELTS/TOEFL/
PTE
科目 all

Her argument is grounded on fact.
她的论点是基于事实的。

fade

（使）褪色；逐渐消失

v. ［feɪd］

考试 TOEFL/IELTS/PTE
科目 listening

All colour fades — especially under the impact of direct sunlight.
所有颜色都会褪色——尤其是在阳光直射下。

fair

公平的，合理的；适当的

adj. ［feə(r)］

考试 KET/PET/IELTS/TOEFL/PTE
科目 all

It didn't seem fair to leave out her father.
将她父亲排除在外似乎不公平。

集市，交易会

n. ［feə(r)］

考试 KET/PET/IELTS/TOEFL/PTE
科目 all

Every autumn I go to the county fair.
每年秋天，我都会去县里的集市。

fall

跌倒；下降；减弱；坠落；开始变成；属于

v. ［fɔːl］

考试 KET/PET/IELTS/TOEFL/PTE
科目 all

The temperature fell sharply in the night.
夜间温度陡降。

秋季

n. ［fɔːl］

考试 KET/PET/IELTS/TOEFL/PTE
科目 all

He was elected judge in the fall of 1991.
他在 1991 年的秋天当选法官。

false

错误的；虚伪的；伪造的，假的

adj. ［fɔːls］

考试 KET/PET/IELTS/TOEFL/
PTE
科目 all

She bowed her head and smiled in false modesty.
她低着头，故作谦卑地笑着。

familiar

熟悉的；通晓的；亲密的；常见的

adj. ［fəˈmɪliə(r)］

F

考试 KET/PET/IELTS/TOEFL/
PTE
科目 all

They are already familiar faces on our TV screens.
他们已经是我们电视屏幕上的熟面孔了。

fan

扇子，风扇；迷，狂热爱好者

n. ［fæn］

考试 KET/PET/IELTS/TOEFL/
PTE
科目 all

He cools himself in front of an electric fan.
他在一个电扇前面吹凉。

扇，扇动；激起

v. ［fæn］

考试 KET/PET/IELTS/TOEFL/
PTE
科目 all

Fanned by a westerly wind, the fire spread rapidly
through the city.
火借助西风迅速蔓延全城。

fantastic

极好的；极大的；难以相信，异想天开的

adj. ［fænˈtæstɪk］

考试 KET/PET/IELTS/TOEFL/
PTE
科目 all

I have a fantastic social life.
我的社交生活丰富多彩。

fascinate

深深吸引，迷住

v. [ˈfæsɪneɪt]

考试 TOEFL/IELTS/PTE
科目 reading

She fascinated him, both on and off stage.
不管是台上还是台下的她，都让他着迷。

fashion

流行式样；时尚，时兴；样子，方式

n. [ˈfæʃn]

考试 KET/PET/IELTS/TOEFL/PTE
科目 all

Fashions in art and literature come and go.
文艺的潮流总是昙花一现。

fasten

扎牢，使固定，扣紧，系牢

v. [ˈfɑːsn]

考试 TOEFL/IELTS/PTE
科目 reading

Her long fair hair was fastened at the nape of her neck by an elastic band.
她用皮筋将金色长发扎在脑后。

fatigue

疲劳；（金属或木材的）疲劳

n. [fəˈtiːg]

考试 TOEFL/IELTS/PTE
科目 reading

Driver fatigue was to blame for the accident.
这次事故是驾驶员疲劳所致。

feasible

可行的，可信的

adj. [ˈfiːzəbl]

考试 TOEFL/IELTS/PTE
科目 listening

This committee selected the plan that seemed most feasible.
委员会选择了那个似乎最切实可行的方案。

fee

费，报名费，会费

n. [fiː]

考试 KET/PET/IELTS/TOEFL/
PTE
科目 all

He hadn't paid his television licence fee.
他尚未缴纳电视机使用许可费。

feed

喂养；饲养；供给，供应

v. [fiːd]

考试 KET/PET/IELTS/TOEFL/
PTE
科目 all

The electricity line is fed with power through an underground cable.
这条电线的电源是通过地下电缆传输的。

feedback

反馈

n. ['fiːdbæk]

考试 TOEFL/IELTS/PTE
科目 reading

I was getting great feedback from my boss.
老板对我的评价很高。

feeling

感情；心情；知觉；同情

n. ['fiːlɪŋ]

考试 KET/PET/IELTS/TOEFL/
PTE
科目 all

He was prompted to a rare outburst of feeling.
他被惹得情绪非常激动，这很少见。

fell

击倒；打倒（某人）；砍伐

vt. [fel]

考试 KET/PET/IELTS/TOEFL/
PTE
科目 all

Badly infected trees should be felled and burned.
感染严重的树木应该砍倒焚烧。

festival

节日；会演，节

n. [ˈfestɪvl]

考试 KET/PET/IELTS/TOEFL/PTE
科目 all

The biggest festival in my country is the Spring Festival.

我国最盛大的节日是春节。

fiction

虚构的事，假想之物；小说

n. [ˈfɪkʃn]

考试 KET/PET/IELTS/TOEFL/PTE
科目 all

Immigrant tales have always been popular themes in fiction.

移民故事一直是小说中常见的主题。

field

田野；运动场；（电或磁）场；领域，范围

n. [fiːld]

考试 KET/PET/IELTS/TOEFL/PTE
科目 all

They went for walks together in the fields.

他们一起在田野里漫步。

figure

体形；轮廓，（隐约可见的）人影；数字；图形

n. [ˈfɪɡə(r)]

考试 KET/PET/IELTS/TOEFL/PTE
科目 all

A figure in a blue dress appeared in the doorway.

一个穿着蓝色连衣裙的身影出现在门口。

描绘；计算；推测；认为；认定

v. [ˈfɪɡə(r)]

考试 KET/PET/IELTS/TOEFL/PTE
科目 all

We figured the sensible thing to do was wait.

我们判定，明智的做法是等待。

film

电影；胶片；薄膜，薄层

n. [fɪlm]

考试 KET/PET/IELTS/TOEFL/PTE
科目 all

Everything was covered in a film of dust.

所有的东西都蒙上了一层灰尘。

拍摄电影

v. [fɪlm]

考试 KET/PET/IELTS/TOEFL/PTE
科目 all

He had filmed her life story.

他把她一生的经历拍成了电影。

final

最终的；决定性的

adj. ['faɪnl]

考试 KET/PET/IELTS/TOEFL/PTE
科目 all

You must have been on stage until the final curtain.

你肯定在台上一直待到了演出结束。

结局；决赛；期末考试

n. ['faɪnl]

考试 TOEFL/IELTS/PTE
科目 listening

Poland know they have a chance of qualifying for the World Cup Finals.

波兰队知道他们有机会获得参加世界杯决赛的资格。

finally

最后，最终；决定性地

adv. ['faɪnəli]

考试 TOEFL/IELTS/PTE
科目 listening

The word was finally given for us to get on board.

终于通知我们登机了。

F

financial

财政的，金融的，财务的

adj. ［faɪˈnænʃl］

考试 TOEFL/IELTS/PTE
科目 reading

The company is in financial difficulties.
公司目前处于财务困难之中。

fine

晴朗的；美好的；纤细的

adj. ［faɪn］

考试 KET/PET/IELTS/TOEFL/PTE
科目 all

There is a fine view of the countryside.
这里可以看到乡村的美景。

对……处以罚款

vt. ［faɪn］

考试 KET/PET/IELTS/TOEFL/PTE
科目 all

Britain and France pursue and fine the consumers of pirated content.
英国和法国追捕盗版内容的消费者，并对其处以罚款。

罚金，罚款

n. ［faɪn］

考试 KET/PET/IELTS/TOEFL/PTE
科目 all

There is a heavy fine for driving drunk.
酒后开车的罚款很重。

finger

手指；指状物；指针

n. ［ˈfɪŋɡə(r)］

考试 KET/PET/IELTS/TOEFL/PTE
科目 all

She ran her fingers through her hair.
她用手指捋了捋头发。

finish

完成；结束；抛光

n. ['fɪnɪʃ]

考试 KET/PET/IELTS/TOEFL/PTE
科目 all

I intend to continue it and see the job through to the finish.

我打算继续下去，直到工作彻底完成。

完成；结束；用完

v. ['fɪnɪʃ]

考试 KET/PET/IELTS/TOEFL/PTE
科目 all

As soon as he'd finished eating, he excused himself.

他一吃完就告辞离开了。

firework

爆竹，花炮；烟火，烟花

n. ['faɪəwɜːk]

考试 KET/PET/IELTS/TOEFL/PTE
科目 all

They drank champagne, set off fireworks and tooted their car horns.

他们喝香槟、放烟花，还按他们的车喇叭。

firm

坚固的；坚决的，坚定的

adj. [fɜːm]

考试 KET/PET/IELTS/TOEFL/PTE
科目 all

Fruit should be firm and in excellent condition.

水果应该硬实完好。

公司，商号

n. [fɜːm]

考试 KET/PET/IELTS/TOEFL/PTE
科目 all

The firm's employees were expecting large bonuses.

这家公司的雇员期待着发放大笔奖金。

F

fix

（使）固定；修理；安装；决定；注视

vt. ［fɪks］

考试 KET/PET/IELTS/TOEFL/
PTE
科目 all

They fixed up the house before they moved in.
他们把房子装修了以后才迁入。

困境

n. ［fɪks］

考试 KET/PET/IELTS/TOEFL/
PTE
科目 all

The government has really got itself into a fix.
政府确实让自己陷入了困境。

---

flee

逃走；逃避

v. ［fliː］

考试 TOEFL/IELTS
科目 writing

He slammed the bedroom door behind him and fled.
他把卧室房门重重地关上，然后逃跑了。

---

flexibility

柔韧，灵活性

n. ［ˌfleksəˈbɪləti］

考试 TOEFL/IELTS/PTE
科目 reading

The flexibility of the lens decreases with age.
眼球晶状体的柔韧性随着年龄的增长而减退。

---

flourish

繁荣；挥舞；茁壮成长

vt. ［ˈflʌrɪʃ］

考试 TOEFL/IELTS
科目 writing

Racism and crime still flourish in the ghetto.
城市贫民区的种族主义和犯罪仍然十分猖獗。

forbid

禁止，不许

vt. ［fə'bɪd］

考试 KET/PET/IELTS/TOEFL/
PTE
科目 all

She was shut away and forbidden to read.
她被关了起来，并且不允许看书。

foretell

预告，预言

vt. ［fɔː'tel］

考试 TOEFL/IELTS
科目 writing

You will never foretell what will happen tomorrow.
你永远都无法预知明天将会发生的事情。

forever

永远；总是

v. ［fər'evə(r)］

考试 KET/PET/IELTS/TOEFL/
PTE
科目 all

I think that we will live together forever.
我想我们会永远生活在一起。

forward

向前

adv. ［'fɔːwəd］

考试 KET/PET/IELTS/TOEFL/
PTE
科目 all

Looking forward, we hope to expand our operations in several of our overseas branches.
展望未来，我们希望拓展其中几家海外分公司的业务。

向前的，前进的；前部的，前面的

adj. ［'fɔːwəd］

考试 KET/PET/IELTS/TOEFL/
PTE
科目 all

Reinforcements were needed to allow more troops to move to forward positions.
需要增援以便让更多的部队推进至前沿阵地。

F

发送；转交

v. ['fɔːwəd]

考试 KET/PET/IELTS/TOEFL/PTE
科目 all

We will forward your letters to him.
我们会把您的信转交给他。

foster

养育；收养；鼓励；促进；助长

v. ['fɒstə(r)]

考试 TOEFL/IELTS/PTE
科目 reading

The club's aim is to foster better relations within the community.
俱乐部的宗旨是促进团体内部的关系。

foundation

基础，根本；建立，创立；地基；基金；基金会

n. [faun'deɪʃn]

考试 TOEFL/IELTS/PTE
科目 reading

Stability is the foundation of continual growth.
稳定是增长得以持续的基础。

freeze

（使）结冰，（使）凝固

v. [friːz]

考试 KET/PET/IELTS/TOEFL/PTE
科目 all

It's so cold that even the river has frozen.
天气冷得河都封冻了。

fresh

新鲜的；无经验的

adj. [freʃ]

考试 KET/PET/IELTS/TOEFL/PTE
科目 all

These foods include fresh fruits and vegetables.
这些食物包括新鲜蔬菜和水果。

fulfil

完成；履行

vt. ［fʊlˈfɪl］

考试 TOEFL/IELTS/PTE
科目 reading

Go and fulfil your promise immediately.

行动起来履行你的承诺。

fulfillment

完成，成就

n. ［fʊlˈfɪlmənt］

考试 TOEFL/IELTS/PTE
科目 reading

We're always reaching for 100 percent happiness and fulfillment.

我们总是追求百分百的快乐和成就。

fully

完全地，彻底地；整整，足足

adv. ［ˈfʊli］

考试 KET/PET/IELTS/TOEFL/
PTE
科目 all

The disease affects fully 30 percent of the population.

这种疾病感染了足足30%的人口。

F

G

gallery

画廊，美术品陈列室；剧场顶层

n. [ˈɡæləri]

考试 KET/PET/IELTS/TOEFL/PTE
科目 all

The painting is in the gallery upstairs.
那幅画在楼上的画廊里。

garage

车库；飞机库；修车厂

n. [ˈɡærɑːʒ]

考试 KET/PET/IELTS/TOEFL/PTE
科目 all

Our garage became my warehouse.
我们家的车库成了我的仓库。

garbage

垃圾，废物

n. [ˈɡɑːbɪdʒ]

考试 KET/PET/IELTS/TOEFL/PTE
科目 all

Don't forget to take out the garbage.
别忘了把垃圾拿出去。

general

一般的，普通的；总的，大体的

adj. [ˈdʒenrəl]

考试 KET/PET/IELTS/TOEFL/PTE
科目 all

The figures represent a general decline in employment.
这些数字显示就业人数总体在下降。

将军

n. [ˈdʒenrəl]

考试 KET/PET/IELTS/TOEFL/
PTE
科目 all

The general assigned him to do the tough task.
将军派他去完成这项艰巨的任务。

genuine

真正的，名副其实的；真诚的

adj. [ˈdʒenjuɪn]

G

考试 TOEFL/IELTS/PTE
科目 reading

Fake designer watches are sold at a fraction of the price of the genuine article.
假冒名牌手表以真品若干分之一的价格出售。

gift

礼品，赠品；天赋，才能

n. [ɡɪft]

考试 KET/PET/IELTS/TOEFL/
PTE
科目 all

As a youth he discovered a gift for teaching.
他年轻时就表现出了教学天赋。

global

全世界的，全球的；整体的，全面的，综合的

adj. [ˈɡləʊbl]

考试 KET/PET/IELTS/TOEFL/
PTE
科目 all

The commission is calling for a global ban on whaling.
委员会要求全球禁止捕鲸。

globe

球体，地球仪；地球，世界

n. [ɡləʊb]

考试 KET/PET/IELTS/TOEFL/
PTE
科目 all

The silvery globe of the moon hung in the sky.
银盘似的月亮悬挂在空中。

glove

手套

n. ［glʌv］

考试 KET/PET/IELTS/TOEFL/PTE
科目 all

He stuck his gloves in his pocket.
他把手套塞进了口袋里。

glue

胶，胶水

n. ［gluː］

考试 KET/PET/IELTS/TOEFL/PTE
科目 all

Once the hot glue dries, the models are done!
等到热胶变干，这些模型就做好了！

粘贴，粘牢

vt. ［gluː］

考试 KET/PET/IELTS/TOEFL/PTE
科目 all

Glue the two pieces of cardboard together.
把这两张硬纸板粘在一起。

gold

金，黄金；金币；金黄色

n. ［ɡəʊld］

考试 KET/PET/IELTS/TOEFL/PTE
科目 all

The price of gold was going up.
黄金的价格在上涨。

金色的

adj. ［ɡəʊld］

考试 KET/PET/IELTS/TOEFL/PTE
科目 all

People dressed in gold and things like that, pretending to be statues.
人们穿上金色的服装和类似的东西，假装是一尊尊雕像。

golden

金的，金质的；金黄色的；贵重的；极好的

adj. [ˈɡəʊldən]

考试 KET/PET/IELTS/TOEFL/ PTE
科目 all

Businesses have a golden opportunity to expand into new markets.

商界有开拓新市场的良机。

good-looking

好看的

adj. [ˌɡʊdˈlʊkɪŋ]

考试 KET/PET/IELTS/TOEFL/ PTE
科目 all

Their study claimed good-looking men and women had higher EQs.

他们的研究声称美貌的人拥有更高的智商。

goods

货物，商品

n. [ɡʊdz]

考试 KET/PET/IELTS/TOEFL/ PTE
科目 all

Money can be exchanged for goods or services.

金钱可以用来换取商品或服务。

government

政府，内阁；治理管理；支配；政体，国家体制

n. [ˈɡʌvənmənt]

考试 KET/PET/IELTS/TOEFL/ PTE
科目 all

The government is responsible for the provision of education for all the children.

政府有责任向所有儿童提供教育。

graduate

大学毕业生，研究生

n. [ˈɡrædʒuət]

考试 KET/PET/IELTS/TOEFL/ PTE
科目 all

He is a graduate of Peking University.

他是北京大学的毕业生。

G

获得学位，大学毕业；授予（某人）学位（或毕业文凭等）

v. ['grædʒueɪt]

考试 KET/PET/IELTS/TOEFL/PTE
科目 all

The university graduated 500 students last year.
该大学去年有 500 名毕业生。

grateful

感激的；感谢的

adj. ['greɪtfl]

考试 KET/PET/IELTS/TOEFL/PTE
科目 all

I am extremely grateful to all the teachers for their help.
我非常感谢所有老师的帮助。

graze

(牲畜) 吃草；放牧；擦伤，擦破

v. [greɪz]

考试 TOEFL/IELTS
科目 writing

The land is used by local people to graze their animals.
这块地当地人用来放牧。

Greece

希腊

n. [griːs]

考试 KET/PET/IELTS/TOEFL/PTE
科目 all

Greece was the cradle of Western culture.
希腊是西方文化的摇篮。

Greek

希腊的

adj. [griːk]

考试 KET/PET/IELTS/TOEFL/PTE
科目 all

Greek yogurt contains much less fat than double cream.
希腊酸奶比高脂浓奶油所含的脂肪要少得多。

希腊人

n. ［griːk］

考试 KET/PET/IELTS/TOEFL/PTE
科目 all

When Greek meets Greek, then comes the tug of war.

希腊人与希腊人相遇，必有一番苦斗（势均力敌，必有激战）。

grey

灰色的

adj. ［greɪ］

考试 KET/PET/IELTS/TOEFL/PTE
科目 all

The ceiling was grey and cracked.

天花板是灰色的，而且有裂纹。

灰色

n. ［greɪ］

考试 KET/PET/IELTS/TOEFL/PTE
科目 all

Maybe her favourite colour is grey.

可能她最喜欢的颜色是灰色吧。

grieve

（使）悲痛，（使）伤心

v. ［griːv］

考试 TOEFL/IELTS
科目 writing

Don't grieve too much for the kitten's death.

别为那只小猫的死过分悲伤。

grip

紧握，抓紧；使感兴趣；使激动；对……产生强有力的影响

v. ［grɪp］

考试 TOEFL/IELTS
科目 writing

She gripped on to the railing with both hands.

她双手紧紧抓住栏杆。

G

ground

地，地面，土地；场地，场所；理由，根据

n. ［graʊnd］

考试 KET/PET/IELTS/TOEFL/PTE
科目 all

He found a purse lying on the ground.

他在地上捡到了一个钱包。

grown-up

成长的，成熟的，成人的

adj. ［ˌɡrəʊnˈʌp］

考试 KET/PET/IELTS/TOEFL/PTE
科目 all

Before you know it, they'll be all grown-up and leaving home.

转眼之间，他们就会长大成人，离开家庭。

成年人

n. ［ˈɡrəʊnʌp］

考试 KET/PET/IELTS/TOEFL/PTE
科目 all

The boy eats like a grown-up.

那个男孩的食量像成人。

growth

生长；增长；发展

n. ［ɡrəʊθ］

考试 KET/PET/IELTS/TOEFL/PTE
科目 all

Lack of food may stunt the growth.

缺乏食物可能妨碍发育。

guarantee

保证，担保；保证单；担保物

n. ［ˌɡærənˈtiː］

考试 TOEFL/IELTS/PTE
科目 reading

The television comes with a year's guarantee.

这台电视机有一年的保修期。

guide

领路人；旅游指南；导游

n. [gaɪd]

考试 KET/PET/IELTS/TOEFL/PTE
科目 all

We've arranged a walking tour of the city with your guide.

我们已安排大家在导游的带领下步行游览这座城市。

领路；指导；支配；管理

vt. [gaɪd]

考试 KET/PET/IELTS/TOEFL/PTE
科目 all

Development has been guided by a concern for the ecology of the area.

该地区的发展以注重生态为指导原则。

guilty

有罪的；内疚的

adj. ['gɪlti]

考试 KET/PET/IELTS/TOEFL/PTE
科目 all

The jury found the defendant not guilty of the offence.

陪审团裁决被告无罪。

guitar

吉他

n. [gɪ'tɑː(r)]

考试 KET/PET/IELTS/TOEFL/PTE
科目 all

He spent his adolescent years playing the guitar in a band.

他在一个乐队里弹吉他，度过了他的青少年时期。

H

hammer

锤子，槌，榔头

n. [ˈhæmə(r)]

考试 KET/PET/IELTS/TOEFL/PTE
科目 all

A hammer is used for driving in nails.
锤子是用来钉钉子的。

锤击，敲打

v. [ˈhæmə(r)]

考试 KET/PET/IELTS/TOEFL/PTE
科目 all

A crowd of reporters was hammering on the door.
一群记者正在砰砰地拍打着门。

handle

柄，把手，拉手

n. [ˈhændl]

考试 TOEFL/IELTS/PTE
科目 reading

I turned the handle and found the door was open.
我转动把手，发现门是开着的。

hang

悬挂，垂吊；吊死，绞死

v. [hæŋ]

考试 KET/PET/IELTS/TOEFL/PTE
科目 all

Don't hang your washing over this line.
别把你洗的衣服晾在这根绳子上。

happen

（偶然）发生；碰巧，恰好

v. [ˈhæpən]

考试 KET/PET/IELTS/TOEFL/
PTE
科目 all

A funny thing happened to me today.

今天我偶然遇到了一件有趣的事。

hardly

几乎不，简直不；仅仅

adv. [ˈhɑːdli]

考试 KET/PET/IELTS/TOEFL/
PTE
科目 all

We ate chips every night, but hardly ever had fish.

我们每晚吃炸薯条，但几乎从不吃鱼。

H

harmonious

和谐的，协调的；和睦的

adj. [hɑːˈməʊniəs]

考试 TOEFL/IELTS/PTE
科目 reading

It is a harmonious community where pupils are happy and industrious.

这是一个和睦的集体，学生们开心玩耍，用功读书。

hasten

催促，赶紧；促进；使加快

v. [ˈheɪsn]

考试 TOEFL/IELTS
科目 writing

The treatment she received may, in fact, have hastened her death.

实际上，她所接受的治疗可能加速了她的死亡。

haul

用力拉，拖

v. [hɔːl]

考试 TOEFL/IELTS
科目 writing

The wagons were hauled by horses.

那些货车是马拉的。

heading

标题；主题

n. [ˈhedɪŋ]

考试 KET/PET/IELTS/TOEFL/PTE
科目 all

The heading was in large letters.
标题是用大号字母印刷的。

heating

加热，供暖

n. [hiːtɪŋ]

考试 KET/PET/IELTS/TOEFL/PTE
科目 all

There is no extra charge for heating.
暖气不另外收费。

heaven

天，天空；天堂

n. [ˈhevn]

考试 KET/PET/IELTS/TOEFL/PTE
科目 all

The island is truly a heaven on earth.
那座岛屿堪称人间天堂。

heed

注意，留心，听从（劝告或警告）

vt. [hiːd]

考试 TOEFL/IELTS
科目 writing

I heeded my doctor's advice and stopped smoking.
我听从医生的劝告，把烟戒了。

heighten

增加，提高；增大；加强

v. [ˈhaɪtn]

考试 TOEFL/IELTS
科目 writing

The campaign is intended to heighten public awareness of the disease.
这场运动的目的是使公众更加了解这种疾病。

hide

隐藏，躲藏；隐瞒

v. [haɪd]

考试 KET/PET/IELTS/TOEFL/
PTE
科目 all

The compound was hidden by trees and shrubs.

大院掩映在树木灌丛之中。

highway

公路，大路，干道

n. [ˈhaɪweɪ]

考试 TOEFL/IELTS/PTE
科目 reading

They're trying to blast away the hill to pave the way for the new highway.

他们试图炸掉这座小山丘来建新公路。

H

hinder

阻碍，阻止

vt. [ˈhɪndə(r)]

考试 TOEFL/IELTS/PTE
科目 reading

Downhearted thoughts hinder progress.

消沉的思想妨碍进步。

hindrance

障碍，妨碍

n. [ˈhɪndrəns]

考试 TOEFL/IELTS/PTE
科目 reading

Adherence to the past is a hindrance.

依附于过去是一种妨碍。

history

历史，历史学；经历

n. [ˈhɪstri]

考试 KET/PET/IELTS/TOEFL/
PTE
科目 all

The value of the history research is to achieve new progress.

史学研究的价值在于取得新进展。

honesty

诚实，正直

n. [ˈɒnəsti]

考试 KET/PET/IELTS/TOEFL/PTE
科目 all

The book isn't, in all honesty, as good as I expected.

说实话，这本书并没有我预期的那么好。

honour

尊敬，敬意；荣誉，光荣

n. [ˈɒnə(r)]

考试 KET/PET/IELTS/TOEFL/PTE
科目 all

Children should be taught to show honour to their parents.

应该教育孩子尊敬父母。

尊敬

v. [ˈɒnə(r)]

考试 KET/PET/IELTS/TOEFL/PTE
科目 all

I honour anyone who listens voluntarily.

我尊敬每一位自发的听众。

horizon

地平线；眼界，见识

n. [həˈraɪzn]

考试 TOEFL/IELTS/PTE
科目 reading

In another fifteen minutes, the sun would begin ascending over the horizon.

再过 15 分钟，太阳就要从地平线升起了。

humorous

富于幽默感的，幽默的；滑稽的

adj. [ˈhjuːmərəs]

考试 KET/PET/IELTS/TOEFL/PTE
科目 all

He had a habit of making humorous remarks.

他有说话幽默的习惯。

I

ignite

点燃；引发

v. [ɪɡ'naɪt]

考试 TOEFL/IELTS
科目 writing

The bombs ignited a fire which destroyed some 60 houses.

炸弹引发的大火烧毁了大约60栋房屋。

image

形象，声誉；印象；画像，雕像；图像；意象，比喻

n. ['ɪmɪdʒ]

考试 KET/PET/IELTS/TOEFL/PTE
科目 all

Images of deer and hunters decorate the cave walls.

洞穴壁上装饰着鹿和猎人的画像。

imagine

想象；设想，料想；猜测

v. [ɪ'mædʒɪn]

考试 KET/PET/IELTS/TOEFL/PTE
科目 all

I can't imagine what has happened.

我想象不出发生了什么事。

imitate

模仿，仿效；仿制，仿造

vt. ['ɪmɪteɪt]

考试 TOEFL/IELTS/PTE
科目 reading

He can imitate his father to the life.

他能惟妙惟肖地模仿他父亲的样子。

immediately

立即；直接地

adv. [ɪˈmiːdiətli]

考试 KET/PET/IELTS/TOEFL/PTE
科目 all

He immediately flung himself to the floor.
他立即飞身扑到地上。

impart

给予；告知，透露；传授

vt. [ɪmˈpɑːt]

考试 TOEFL/IELTS
科目 writing

The spice imparts an Eastern flavour to the dish.
这种调味品给菜肴添加了一种东方风味。

imperative

紧急的，必要的；强制的

adj. [ɪmˈperətɪv]

考试 TOEFL/IELTS/PTE
科目 reading

It is imperative for your recovery to continue the treatment for at least two months.
重要的是你必须继续治疗至少两个月才能恢复健康。

impossibility

不可能的事

n. [ɪmˌpɒsəˈbɪləti]

考试 KET/PET/IELTS/TOEFL/PTE
科目 all

He hinted at the impossibility of winding up the work in two months.
他暗示在两个月内结束这项工作是不可能的。

impress

印，盖印；使铭记，留下印象，引人注目；使钦佩

v. [ɪmˈpres]

考试 KET/PET/IELTS/TOEFL/PTE
科目 all

What impressed him most was their speed.
最令他佩服的是他们的速度。

incentive

刺激；动力；鼓励；诱因；动机

n. ［ɪnˈsentɪv］

考试 TOEFL/IELTS/PTE
科目 reading

There is little or no incentive for people to save fuel.
几乎没有使人们节约燃料的鼓励方法。

inclination

倾向；意愿

n. ［ˌɪnklɪˈneɪʃn］

考试 TOEFL/IELTS/PTE
科目 reading

The car has an inclination to stall on cold mornings.
这辆汽车天冷时早晨常常熄火。

include

包括，包含，计入

vt. ［ɪnˈkluːd］

考试 KET/PET/IELTS/TOEFL/
PTE
科目 all

The trip has been extended to include a few other events.
旅程被延长，其他几项活动也被包括进来了。

inconsistent

不一致的；不符合的

adj. ［ˌɪnkənˈsɪstənt］

考试 TOEFL/IELTS/PTE
科目 listening

Terry's speech was inconsistent with the book he had written.
特里的演讲和他写的书相互矛盾。

incur

招致，遭受

vt. ［ɪnˈkɜː(r)］

考试 TOEFL/IELTS/PTE
科目 reading

She falls in love and incurs the wrath of her father.
她恋爱了，这引起了父亲的愤怒。

indispensable

必需的，必不可少的

adj. [ˌɪndɪˈspensəbl]

Cars have become an indispensable part of our lives.
汽车已经成为我们生活中必不可少的一部分。

indulge

放纵，沉迷于

v. [ɪnˈdʌldʒ]

You can indulge yourself without spending a fortune.
你不必花大把钱就可以好好犒劳一下自己。

industry

工业，产业；行业；勤劳，勤奋

n. [ˈɪndəstri]

That man is a big wheel in the electronics industry.
那位男士是电子工业巨子。

infer

推论，推断

vt. [ɪnˈfɜː(r)]

People usually infer an unknown fact from a known fact.
人们通常从已知的事实中推断未知的事实。

influence

影响，感化；支配力，控制力，影响力

n. [ˈɪnfluəns]

The influence of climate on crops are self-evident.
气候对农作物的影响是不证自明的。

影响；改变；支配

vt. [ˈinfluəns]

考试 KET/PET/IELTS/TOEFL/ PTE
科目 all

My father influenced me to learn English.
我学英语是受父亲的影响。

inherit

继承；遗传而得；成为继承人

v. [ɪnˈherɪt]

考试 TOEFL/IELTS
科目 writing

He has inherited his mother's patience.
这种耐心是母亲遗传给他的。

I

initiative

倡议，新方案；主动权，主动精神；主动性，自发性，积极性

n. [ɪˈnɪʃətɪv]

考试 TOEFL/IELTS/PTE
科目 reading

Government initiatives to help young people have been inadequate.
政府在积极帮助年轻人方面做得还不够。

injure

损害，伤害

vt. [ˈɪndʒə(r)]

考试 KET/PET/IELTS/TOEFL/ PTE
科目 all

Several policemen were injured in the clashes.
几名警察在冲突中受伤。

insist

强调；坚持；坚持说

v. [ɪnˈsɪst]

考试 KET/PET/IELTS/TOEFL/ PTE
科目 all

We insisted on a refund of the full amount.
我们坚决要求全额退款。

inspire

激励，鼓励；赋予灵感；使产生（感觉或情感）

vt. ［ɪnˈspaɪə(r)］

考试科目 TOEFL/IELTS/PTE reading

By visiting schools, the actors hope to inspire children to put on their own productions.
演员们希望通过访问学校鼓励孩子们演出自己的作品。

integral

完整的，完备的；必需的，不可或缺的

adj. ［ˈɪntɪɡrəl］

考试科目 TOEFL/IELTS/PTE reading

Rituals and festivals form an integral part of every human society.
仪式与节日构成了任何人类社会不可缺少的一部分。

intelligence

智力；理解力；情报人员；情报

n. ［ɪnˈtelɪdʒəns］

考试科目 TOEFL/IELTS/PTE reading

These magnificent ancient buildings demonstrate the great intelligence of the labouring people.
这些壮丽的古代建筑显示了劳动人民的高度智慧。

intrude

闯入，侵入，侵扰

vi. ［ɪnˈtruːd］

考试科目 TOEFL/IELTS writing

I don't want to intrude on your meeting.
我不想打扰你们的会议。

invade

侵略，侵犯；涌入，侵袭

v. ［ɪnˈveɪd］

考试科目 TOEFL/IELTS writing

The cancer cells may invade other parts of the body.
癌细胞可能扩散到身体的其他部位。

invasion

入侵，侵略；侵犯；侵袭

n. [ɪnˈveɪʒn]

考试 TOEFL/IELTS/PTE
科目 reading

He advised them how to stop the invasion.
他给他们出主意怎样阻止入侵。

invest

投资，购买；授予；耗费；投入

v. [ɪnˈvest]

考试 TOEFL/IELTS/PTE
科目 reading

The government has invested heavily in public transport.
政府已对公共交通投入了大量资金。

I

iron

铁；铁制品；烙铁；熨斗

n. [ˈaɪən]

考试 KET/PET/IELTS/TOEFL/PTE
科目 all

The melting point of copper is not so high as that of iron.
铜的熔点不如铁高。

熨（衣），熨平

v. [ˈaɪən]

考试 KET/PET/IELTS/TOEFL/PTE
科目 all

She's ironing his shirt.
她正在熨烫他的衬衫。

item

条款；项目；一则，一条（新闻）；一件商品（或物品）

n. [ˈaɪtəm]

考试 KET/PET/IELTS/TOEFL/PTE
科目 all

I marked out an item in the list.
我从清单上划掉了一件商品。

J

jam

压紧，夹住；发生故障；塞进

v. [dʒæm]

考试 KET/PET/IELTS/TOEFL/
PTE
科目 all

The cupboards were jammed full of old news-papers.
橱柜里塞满了旧报纸。

阻塞物；窘境；果酱

n. [dʒæm]

考试 KET/PET/IELTS/TOEFL/
PTE
科目 all

Despite the traffic jam he arrived here on time.
尽管交通堵塞，他仍然准时到达这里。

jettison

抛弃，投弃

vt. ['dʒetɪsn]

考试 TOEFL/IELTS
科目 writing

The Government seems to have jettisoned the plan.
政府似乎已经放弃了这个计划。

jewellery

珠宝，珠宝类

n. ['dʒuːəlri]

考试 KET/PET/IELTS/TOEFL/
PTE
科目 all

The robbers carried off the set of jewellery.
强盗劫走了一套珠宝。

jog

轻推，缓步前进，慢跑

v. ［dʒɒg］

考试 KET/PET/IELTS/TOEFL/
PTE
科目 all

Jogging up and down the stairwell or bleachers is a great cardio workout.

沿着楼梯或运动场的露天看台上下慢跑是一项非常有益的有氧运动。

轻推，缓步前进，慢跑

n. ［dʒɒg］

考试 KET/PET/IELTS/TOEFL/
PTE
科目 all

He went for another early morning jog.

他又去晨跑了。

jungle

丛林，密林；危险地带

n. ［ˈdʒʌŋgl］

考试 KET/PET/IELTS/TOEFL/
PTE
科目 all

The area was covered in dense jungle.

这个地区丛林密布。

K

kangaroo

袋鼠

n. ［ˌkæŋɡəˈruː］

考试 KET/PET/IELTS/TOEFL/PTE
科目 all

A kangaroo is an interesting animal.
袋鼠是一种有趣的动物。

keen

锋利的，尖锐的；强烈的；渴望的

adj. ［kiːn］

考试 KET/PET/IELTS/TOEFL/PTE
科目 all

He is always keen to help others.
他总是很热心地帮助别人。

keyboard

键盘

n. ［ˈkiːbɔːd］

考试 KET/PET/IELTS/TOEFL/PTE
科目 all

The computer has a normal QWERTY keyboard.
这台计算机配有标准的键盘。

kindle

开始燃烧，点燃；引起；照亮

v. ［ˈkɪndl］

考试 TOEFL/IELTS
科目 writing

The Second World War kindled his enthusiasm for politics.
第二次世界大战激起了他的政治热情。

L

labour

工作，劳动；劳力；分娩

n. [ˈleɪbə(r)]

考试 KET/PET/IELTS/TOEFL/PTE
科目 all

We regard labour as a matter of honour.
我们认为劳动是光荣的事。

劳动；苦干

vi. [ˈleɪbə(r)]

考试 KET/PET/IELTS/TOEFL/PTE
科目 all

She had laboured late into the night to finish her essay.
为了完成文章，她工作到深夜。

lamb

小羊；羊羔肉

n. [læm]

考试 KET/PET/IELTS/TOEFL/PTE
科目 all

The little lamb was caught by the wolf.
小羊被狼抓住了。

lap

一圈；（坐着时的）大腿部

n. [læp]

考试 KET/PET/IELTS/TOEFL/PTE
科目 all

She waited quietly with her hands in her lap.
她双手放在大腿上静静等候。

领先……一圈（或数圈）；拍打；舔食

v. ［læp］

考试 KET/PET/IELTS/TOEFL/PTE
科目 all

He built a 10-bike lead before lapping his first rider on the 14th lap.

他领先了 10 辆自行车的距离，然后在第 14 圈又超过了前一个车手一圈。

layer

层；层次

n. ［ˈleɪə(r)］

考试 KET/PET/IELTS/TOEFL/PTE
科目 all

A fresh layer of snow covered the street.

街上覆盖了一层新雪。

leak

漏洞；泄漏

n. ［liːk］

考试 KET/PET/IELTS/TOEFL/PTE
科目 all

It's thought a gas leak may have caused the blast.

人们认为可能是煤气泄漏引起了爆炸。

lean

倾斜，屈身；倚，靠；使斜靠

v. ［liːn］

考试 TOEFL/IELTS
科目 writing

The building leaned before it was renovated.

在修复前，那幢楼倾斜着。

left-handed

左手的；左侧的；左撇子的

adj. ［ˌleftˈhændɪd］

考试 KET/PET/IELTS/TOEFL/PTE
科目 all

There is a shop in town that supplies practically everything for left-handed people.

镇上有一家商店，出售左撇子用品。

legend

传说，传奇故事；刻印文字，铭文；图例，说明，解释

n. [ˈledʒənd]

考试 KET/PET/IELTS/TOEFL/PTE
科目 all

The play was based on Irish legend.
这部戏取材于爱尔兰传说。

leisure

空闲，闲暇；安逸

n. [ˈleʒə(r)]

考试 TOEFL/IELTS/PTE
科目 reading

I have no leisure for playing cards.
我没有闲暇玩牌。

lessen

减少，减轻；缩小

v. [ˈlesn]

考试 TOEFL/IELTS
科目 writing

These measures can't help lessen the existing tension.
这些措施不能帮助缓和现在的紧张局势。

L

levy

征收；征税；征集

vt. [ˈlevi]

考试 TOEFL/IELTS
科目 writing

Taxes should not be levied without the authority of Parliament.
未经议会授权不得征税。

lighten

（使）变明亮；（使）轻松；缓和

v. [ˈlaɪtn]

考试 TOEFL/IELTS/PTE
科目 reading

The sky began to lighten.
天空开始变亮了。

lightning

闪电

n. [ˈlaɪtnɪŋ]

考试 KET/PET/IELTS/TOEFL/PTE
科目 all

Thunder and lightning scare most children and many adults.
多数孩子和许多成人恐惧雷鸣和闪电。

闪电般的；快速的

adj. [ˈlaɪtnɪŋ]

考试 KET/PET/IELTS/TOEFL/PTE
科目 all

Driving today demands lightning reflexes.
如今开车需要反应极其迅速。

likelihood

可能性，可能

n. [ˈlaɪklihʊd]

考试 TOEFL/IELTS/PTE
科目 reading

The likelihood of infection is minimal.
传染的可能性微乎其微。

linger

逗留，徘徊；缓慢消失；苟延残喘

vi. [ˈlɪŋgə(r)]

考试 TOEFL/IELTS
科目 writing

A guerrilla war has lingered into its fourth decade.
一场游击战已经持续了 30 多年。

link

连接；联系

vt. [lɪŋk]

考试 KET/PET/IELTS/TOEFL/PTE
科目 all

The study further strengthens the evidence linking smoking with early death.
这项研究进一步证实了吸烟与早逝之间的联系。

环节；链环

n. [lɪŋk]

考试 KET/PET/IELTS/TOEFL/PTE
科目 all

We must take firm hold the key link of our work.
我们要牢牢抓住工作的主要环节。

livelihood

生活，生计，营生

n. ['laɪvlihʊd]

考试 TOEFL/IELTS/PTE
科目 reading

They depended on animal husbandry for their livelihood.

他们以畜牧业为生。

location

位置，场所；定位

n. [ləʊ'keɪʃn]

考试 KET/PET/IELTS/TOEFL/
PTE
科目 all

The first thing he looked at was his office's location.

他首先看的是自己办公室的位置。

lodge

为（某人）提供住宿；临时住宿；寄宿；寄存

v. [lɒdʒ]

L

考试 TOEFL/IELTS
科目 writing

The building he was lodged in turned out to be a warehouse.

原来，他租住的那栋建筑是一座仓库。

loom

隐隐呈现；赫然耸现；逼近

vi. [luːm]

考试 TOEFL/IELTS
科目 writing

The mountainous island loomed on the horizon.

那座巨大的岛屿隐隐约约浮现在地平线上。

lounge

懒洋洋地站（或坐、躺）着

vi. [laʊndʒ]

考试 TOEFL/IELTS
科目 writing

Laura lounged in the hammock.

劳拉懒洋洋地躺在吊床里。

M

machine

机器，机械；机构

n. [məˈʃiːn]

考试 KET/PET/IELTS/TOEFL/PTE
科目 all

This machine goes by electricity.

这台机器是由电力推动的。

（用机器）制造，加工成型

v. [məˈʃiːn]

考试 KET/PET/IELTS/TOEFL/PTE
科目 all

The material is machined in a factory.

这种材料在一家工厂里用机器加工成型。

magazine

杂志；期刊；弹药库；弹盒

n. [ˌmæɡəˈziːn]

考试 KET/PET/IELTS/TOEFL/PTE
科目 all

He writes short stories for a monthly magazine.

他为一家月刊杂志撰写短篇小说。

magic

魔术；魔法；巫术

n. [ˈmædʒɪk]

考试 KET/PET/IELTS/TOEFL/PTE
科目 all

They believe in magic.

他们相信巫术。

有魔力的；神奇的，不可思议的

adj. ['mædʒɪk]

考试 KET/PET/IELTS/TOEFL/
PTE
科目 all

There is no magic formula for passing exams —
only hard work.
根本没有通过考试的魔法，只有勤奋学习。

magnify

放大；赞美；夸大，夸张

vt. ['mæɡnɪfaɪ]

考试 TOEFL/IELTS
科目 writing

A lens would magnify the picture so it would be like
looking at a large TV screen.
透镜会把图片放大，就像在看巨大的电视屏幕一样。

maintenance

维修；维持，保持；生活费

n. ['meɪntənəns]

考试 TOEFL/IELTS/PTE
科目 reading

The window was replaced last week during routine
maintenance.
上周例行维修的时候换了窗户。

M

Malaysia

马来西亚

n. [mə'leɪʒə]

考试 KET/PET/IELTS/TOEFL/
PTE
科目 all

Port Klang is the biggest port in Malaysia.
巴生港是马来西亚最大的港口。

manager

经理，管理人员

n. ['mænɪdʒə(r)]

考试 KET/PET/IELTS/TOEFL/
PTE
科目 all

He is incompetent as manager of the hotel.
他没有能力当那家旅馆的经理。

manufacturer

生产者；制作者；制造商

n. ［ˌmænju'fæktʃərə(r)］

考试 TOEFL/IELTS/PTE
科目 reading

The manufacturer's name is on the bottom of the plate.
制造厂商的名称在盘子背面。

march

（使）行军，（使）行进；使同行

v. ［mɑːtʃ］

考试 KET/PET/IELTS/TOEFL/PTE
科目 all

They marched shoulder to shoulder.
他们并肩前进。

行军，行进；抗议游行

n. ［mɑːtʃ］

考试 KET/PET/IELTS/TOEFL/PTE
科目 all

After a short march, the column entered the village.
短途行军后，队伍进了村。

market

集市，市场；交易；销路；需求

n. ［'mɑːkɪt］

考试 KET/PET/IELTS/TOEFL/PTE
科目 all

He shot quail for the market.
他把打下的鹌鹑卖到集市上去。

推销；销售；促销

vt. ［'mɑːkɪt］

考试 KET/PET/IELTS/TOEFL/PTE
科目 all

Touch-tone telephones have been marketed in America since 1963.
按键式电话从 1963 年起就开始在美国销售。

mask

面具；口罩；掩饰

n. [mɑːsk]

考试 KET/PET/IELTS/TOEFL/
PTE
科目 all

This gas mask can immunize you against poison gas.
防毒面具能使你免遭毒气袭击。

遮蔽，伪装

vt. [mɑːsk]

考试 KET/PET/IELTS/TOEFL/
PTE
科目 all

Her smile masked true feelings.
她的微笑掩饰了她的感情。

massive

厚重的；大量的；大规模的

adj. ['mæsɪv]

考试 TOEFL/IELTS/PTE
科目 reading

The world's largest public square has been turned
into a massive garden.
世界上最大的广场已经变成了一个巨大的花园。

M

master

主人；师父；硕士

n. ['mɑːstə(r)]

考试 KET/PET/IELTS/TOEFL/
PTE
科目 all

My master ordered me not to deliver the message
except in private.
我的主人命令我务必私下里传递消息。

精通；控制；征服

vt. ['mɑːstə(r)]

考试 KET/PET/IELTS/TOEFL/
PTE
科目 all

Students are expected to master a second
language.
学生们应该掌握一门第二语言。

最重要的；最大的；熟练的

adj. [ˈmɑːstə(r)]

考试 KET/PET/IELTS/TOEFL/PTE
科目 all

My husband decided to install a light switch in our master bedroom.

我丈夫决定在我们的主卧室里安装一个电灯开关。

material

材料，原料，布料

n. [məˈtɪəriəl]

考试 KET/PET/IELTS/TOEFL/PTE
科目 all

The material must be moderately coherent and firm.

材料必须有适度的黏着力和坚固性。

物质的；实质性的；重要的

adj. [məˈtɪəriəl]

考试 KET/PET/IELTS/TOEFL/PTE
科目 all

Every room must have been stuffed with material things.

每个房间肯定都塞满了东西。

materialism

唯物主义，唯物论；实利主义，物质主义

n. [məˈtɪəriəlɪzəm]

考试 TOEFL/IELTS/PTE
科目 reading

Thai culture blends buddhism, spirit beliefs and materialism.

泰国文化混合了佛教、精神信仰和唯物主义。

medal

奖章，纪念章，勋章

n. [ˈmedl]

考试 KET/PET/IELTS/TOEFL/PTE
科目 all

The government recognized his outstanding service by giving him a medal.

政府为他颁赠勋章，以表彰他的卓著功绩。

medical

医学的，医药的；内科的

adj. [ˈmedɪkl]

考试 KET/PET/IELTS/TOEFL/
PTE
科目 all

Advances in medical science have made it possible
to cure many so-called obstinate illnesses.
医学的发达使很多所谓的痼疾都能治好。

meditate

考虑，沉思；冥想；计划；企图

v. [ˈmedɪteɪt]

考试 TOEFL/IELTS
科目 writing

I meditate in order to relax.
我沉思冥想以得到放松。

medium

媒介；形式；介质

n. [ˈmiːdiəm]

考试 KET/PET/IELTS/TOEFL/
PTE
科目 all

Commercial television is an effective medium for
advertising.
商业电视是有效的广告宣传工具。

中等的，中号的

adj. [ˈmiːdiəm]

考试 KET/PET/IELTS/TOEFL/
PTE
科目 all

A medium dose produces severe nausea within
hours.
中等剂量几小时之内会引发严重的恶心。

melt

融化；（使）熔化

v. [melt]

考试 KET/PET/IELTS/TOEFL/
PTE
科目 all

His enthusiasm is enough to melt a heart of stone.
他的热诚足以软化铁石心肠。

M

membership

成员资格，会员身份；成员，会员

n. [ˈmembəʃɪp]

考试 KET/PET/IELTS/TOEFL/PTE
科目 all

She had allowed her membership to lapse.
她的会员资格期满终止，没有再续。

mend

修理，缝补；改正，改进；愈合

v. [mend]

考试 KET/PET/IELTS/TOEFL/PTE
科目 all

Can you mend this broken chair?
你能修理这把破椅子吗？

mention

提及，谈到

vt. [ˈmenʃn]

考试 KET/PET/IELTS/TOEFL/PTE
科目 all

He forbears to mention the matter again.
他克制自己，不再提及此事。

提及，说起

n. [ˈmenʃn]

考试 KET/PET/IELTS/TOEFL/PTE
科目 all

I've never come across any mention of him.
我从来没听人说起过他。

merit

价值；优点；功绩

n. [ˈmerɪt]

考试 TOEFL/IELTS/PTE
科目 reading

I don't think there's much merit in the plan.
我认为这项计划没什么价值。

mess

凌乱；混乱的局面；困境；食堂，餐厅

n. ［mes］

考试 KET/PET/IELTS/TOEFL/ PTE
科目 all
I do beg your pardon for the mess I've made.
我把事情搞得一团糟，请您原谅。

弄乱；弄糟，弄脏；随地便溺

v. ［mes］

考试 KET/PET/IELTS/TOEFL/ PTE
科目 all
The late arrival of the train messed up all our plans.
火车晚点把我们的计划全打乱了。

metal

金属，金属制品

n. ［'metl］

考试 KET/PET/IELTS/TOEFL/ PTE
科目 all
A hammer has a metal head and a wooden or metal handle.
锤子有个金属做的头以及一个木头或金属做的柄。

M

method

方法，办法；条理

n. ［'meθəd］

考试 KET/PET/IELTS/TOEFL/ PTE
科目 all
His working method is relatively simple.
他的工作方法相对简单。

Mexican

墨西哥人

n. ［'meksɪkən］

考试 KET/PET/IELTS/TOEFL/ PTE
科目 all
He went down the bar to a group of Mexicans and talked to them in a low voice.
他走到酒吧里的一群墨西哥人那里，跟他们小声交谈起来。

墨西哥（人）的

adj. [ˈmeksɪkən]

考试 KET/PET/IELTS/TOEFL/PTE
科目 all

The Mexican government has also started an investigation.
墨西哥政府也已经开始调查此事了。

Mexico

墨西哥

n. [ˈmeksɪkəʊ]

考试 KET/PET/IELTS/TOEFL/PTE
科目 all

Mexico suffered more drug violence.
墨西哥的毒品暴力活动再起波澜。

microwave

微波

n. [ˈmaɪkrəweɪv]

考试 KET/PET/IELTS/TOEFL/PTE
科目 all

Microwave ovens can also disrupt your wireless signal.
微波炉可能也会干扰你的无线信号。

mile

英里；较大的距离

n. [maɪl]

考试 KET/PET/IELTS/TOEFL/PTE
科目 all

The area had a population density of five people per square mile.
该地区人口密度为每平方英里五人。

military

军事的，军人的，军队的

adj. [ˈmɪlətri]

考试 TOEFL/IELTS/PTE
科目 reading

Military action may become necessary.
也许有必要采取军事行动。

million

百万；大量

num.　[ˈmɪljən]

考试 KET/PET/IELTS/TOEFL/
PTE
科目 all

Up to five million people a year visit the county.

每年参观这个县的人多达 500 万。

---

millionaire

百万富翁；大富豪

n.　[ˌmɪljəˈneə(r)]

考试 KET/PET/IELTS/TOEFL/
PTE
科目 all

By the time he died, he had been a millionaire.

到他去世的时候，他已经是一位百万富翁了。

---

mince

切碎，绞碎；装腔作势；碎步走

v.　[mɪns]

考试 TOEFL/IELTS
科目 writing

Perhaps I'll buy lean meat and mince it myself.

也许我会买点瘦肉自己绞碎。

M

---

mingle

(使) 混合，交往

v.　[ˈmɪŋgl]

考试 TOEFL/IELTS
科目 writing

You cannot mingle oil and water.

你不能把油和水混合在一起。

---

minimize

使减少到最低限度；极度轻视，小看；使最小化

vt.　[ˈmɪnɪmaiz]

考试 TOEFL/IELTS/PTE
科目 reading

Concerned people want to minimize the risk of developing cancer.

相关人员希望尽可能降低患癌风险。

mixture

考试 KET/PET/IELTS/TOEFL/PTE
科目 all

混合；混合物；混合剂

n. [ˈmɪkstʃə(r)]

Air is a mixture of gases.
空气是气体的混合物。

moderate

考试 TOEFL/IELTS/PTE
科目 reading

适度的，适中的；稳健的，温和的

adj. [ˈmɒdərət]

Moderate exercise subserves digestion.
适度锻炼有助于消化。

modest

考试 KET/PET/IELTS/TOEFL/PTE
科目 all

谦虚的；适度的

adj. [ˈmɒdɪst]

He's modest, as well as being a great player.
他是一名谦虚而伟大的运动员。

moral

考试 TOEFL/IELTS/PTE
科目 reading

道德的；道义上的；品行端正的

adj. [ˈmɒrəl]

He lives by a strict moral code.
他按照严格的道德准则生活。

morale

考试 TOEFL/IELTS/PTE
科目 reading

士气，斗志

n. [məˈrɑːl]

Their morale had greatly improved.
他们的士气大大提高了。

morality

考试 TOEFL/IELTS/PTE
科目 reading

道德，美德；品行

n. [məˈræləti]

The morality they absorbed was beyond question.
他们的道德无可置疑。

motivation

动机；积极性

n. [ˌməʊtɪ'veɪʃn]

考试 TOEFL/IELTS/PTE
科目 reading

Without direction and motivation a person would not know what to do.

一个人缺乏方向和动力就不知道该干些什么。

motorcar

汽车

n. ['məʊtəkɑː]

考试 KET/PET/IELTS/TOEFL/PTE
科目 all

There is keen competition between the two motorcar firms.

两家汽车公司之间存在着激烈的竞争。

motorcycle

摩托车

n. ['məʊtəsaɪkl]

考试 KET/PET/IELTS/TOEFL/PTE
科目 all

He rode a motorcycle to the station.

他骑摩托车去车站。

mud

泥，泥浆

n. [mʌd]

考试 KET/PET/IELTS/TOEFL/PTE
科目 all

His clothes were dashed with mud.

他的衣服溅上了泥。

弄脏，使沾污泥

vt. [mʌd]

考试 KET/PET/IELTS/TOEFL/PTE
科目 all

She mudded herself when running in the rain.

她在雨中奔跑时溅了自己一身泥。

muse

沉思，冥想

v. [mjuːz]

考试 TOEFL/IELTS
科目 writing

The young girl was musing on the events of the day.

这个女孩在沉思一天中所发生的事。

M

museum

博物馆

n. ［mjuːˈziəm］

The museum has many immemorial cultural relics.
该博物馆收藏了很多古老的文物。

mushroom

蘑菇

n. ［ˈmʌʃrʊm］

There are many types of wild mushrooms.
野生蘑菇有很多种。

迅速发展；采蘑菇

vi. ［ˈmʌʃrʊm］

The media training industry has mushroomed over the past decade.
在过去的 10 年里，媒体培训产业发展迅猛。

mutter

轻声低语；喃喃自语

v. ［ˈmʌtə(r)］

He muttered a few words of apology and with that he left.
他支支吾吾地道个歉就走了。

mystery

神秘，神秘的事物；悬疑小说（或电影、戏剧）

n. ［ˈmɪstri］

This mystery puzzles me.
这件神秘的事情让我百思不解。

N

naive

天真的；幼稚的；轻信的

adj. [naɪˈiːv]

考试 KET/PET/IELTS/TOEFL/ PTE
科目 all

Children always ask naive questions.
小孩子总是问天真的问题。

napkin

餐巾，餐巾纸；尿布

n. [ˈnæpkɪn]

考试 KET/PET/IELTS/TOEFL/ PTE
科目 all

The mother laid a piece of napkin under the baby's body.
这位母亲在婴儿的身体下面铺了一块尿布。

national

民族的，国家的

adj. [ˈnæʃnəl]

考试 KET/PET/IELTS/TOEFL/ PTE
科目 all

Baseball is the national pastime.
棒球是全民性的休闲运动。

navy

海军；深蓝色

n. [ˈneɪvi]

考试 KET/PET/IELTS/TOEFL/ PTE
科目 all

He is an officer in the navy.
他是一名海军军官。

necessity

必要性，需要；必然性；必需品

n. [nə'sesəti]

考试 TOEFL/IELTS/PTE
科目 reading

There is agreement on the necessity of reforms.
对改革的必要性已经达成了共识。

necklace

项链；项圈

n. ['nekləs]

考试 KET/PET/IELTS/TOEFL/
PTE
科目 all

My necklace is made of pure gold.
我的项链是纯金的。

negative

否定的；消极的；阴性的

adj. ['negətɪv]

考试 KET/PET/IELTS/TOEFL/
PTE
科目 all

He gave me a negative answer.
他给了我一个否定的答案。

否定；底片

n. ['negətɪv]

考试 KET/PET/IELTS/TOEFL/
PTE
科目 all

Photo negatives smudge easily.
照片底片很容易变脏。

neighbourhood

邻近的地方；街区

n. ['neɪbəhʊd]

考试 KET/PET/IELTS/TOEFL/
PTE
科目 all

He gathered the boys and girls of the neighbourhood for a picnic.
他把街坊邻居的孩子们都聚拢来一起野餐。

nerve

神经；勇气

n. [nɜːrv]

考试 KET/PET/IELTS/TOEFL/PTE
科目 all

He never got up enough nerve to meet me.
他从来没有足够的胆量来见我。

nervous

神经质的；焦虑的，紧张不安的；神经系统的

adj. [ˈnɜːvəs]

考试 KET/PET/IELTS/TOEFL/PTE
科目 all

The number of nervous disorders was rising in the region.
该地区神经紊乱患者的人数在上升。

noisy

吵闹的，喧闹的

adj. [ˈnɔɪzi]

考试 KET/PET/IELTS/TOEFL/PTE
科目 all

The local inhabitants do not like noisy tourists in summer.
当地居民不喜欢夏季喧闹的游客。

N

norm

常态；标准；规范；定额

n. [nɔːm]

考试 TOEFL/IELTS/PTE
科目 reading

Quarterly reporting is already the norm in this company.
在这家公司，季度业绩报告已成为常规。

notion

概念；见解；打算

n. [ˈnəʊʃn]

考试 TOEFL/IELTS/PTE
科目 reading

She had only a vague notion of what might happen.
对于可能发生的事她只有一个模糊的概念。

nurse

护士；保姆

n. ［nɜːs］

考试 KET/PET/IELTS/TOEFL/PTE
科目 all

She has spent 29 years as a nurse.

她做了 29 年的护士。

护理，看护；当保姆；哺育

v. ［nɜːs］

考试 KET/PET/IELTS/TOEFL/PTE
科目 all

All the years he was sick my mother had nursed him.

在他生病的那些年里，我母亲一直在照顾他。

---

nursery

托儿所，保育室；苗圃

n. ［ˈnɜːsəri］

考试 KET/PET/IELTS/TOEFL/PTE
科目 all

She resigned her children to the care of the nursery.

她把孩子们交给托儿所照管。

O

obey

服从，顺从

v. [ə'beɪ]

考试 KET/PET/IELTS/TOEFL/
PTE
科目 all

Most people obey the law.
大多数人都遵纪守法。

oblige

迫使；帮……的忙，效劳；使感激

v. [ə'blaɪdʒ]

考试 TOEFL/IELTS
科目 writing

This decree obliges unions to delay strikes.
该法令迫使工会推迟罢工。

ocean

海洋；（五大洋之一的）洋

n. ['əʊʃn]

考试 KET/PET/IELTS/TOEFL/
PTE
科目 all

Our beach house is just a couple of miles from the ocean.
我家滨海的房子离大海只有几英里。

offend

冒犯，得罪；使厌恶；违反；犯罪，犯法

v. [ə'fend]

考试 KET/PET/IELTS/TOEFL/
PTE
科目 all

I don't mean to offend you.
我不是故意冒犯你的。

offer

提出；提供，供应

v. [ˈɒfə(r)]

考试 KET/PET/IELTS/TOEFL/PTE
科目 all

The number of companies offering them work increased.
越来越多的公司向他们提供工作机会。

提供；出价

n. [ˈɒfə(r)]

考试 KET/PET/IELTS/TOEFL/PTE
科目 all

He had refused several excellent job offers.
他已经拒绝了好几个绝佳的工作机会。

offering

用品；作品；供品

n. [ˈɒfərɪŋ]

考试 TOEFL/IELTS
科目 writing

It was very, very good, far better than vegetarian offerings in many a posh restaurant.
这道菜真是人间美味，远远超过很多豪华餐厅的素食菜品。

officer

官员，办事员；工作人员；军官

n. [ˈɒfɪsə(r)]

考试 KET/PET/IELTS/TOEFL/PTE
科目 all

The officer ordered that all the soldiers get ready.
军官命令所有士兵做好准备。

offset

抵消，补偿

vt. [ˈɒfset]

考试 TOEFL/IELTS
科目 writing

Her virtues offset her fault.
她的美德弥补了她的缺点。

onion

洋葱

n. [ˈʌnjən]

考试 KET/PET/IELTS/TOEFL/PTE
科目 all

She sliced the onion and put it in the beef stew.
她将洋葱切片放入炖牛肉中。

operate

操作，运转；开动；起作用；动手术

v. [ˈɒpəreɪt]

考试 KET/PET/IELTS/TOEFL/PTE
科目 all

The machines will not operate properly.
那些机器不能正常运转。

operation

操作；手术；运算，运作；经营

n. [ˌɒpəˈreɪʃn]

考试 KET/PET/IELTS/TOEFL/PTE
科目 all

The filter is now ready for operation.
这种滤器目前即将投入运转。

opinion

意见，主张

n. [əˈpɪnjən]

O

考试 KET/PET/IELTS/TOEFL/PTE
科目 all

I'm interested in your opinion.
我对你的想法很感兴趣。

opportunity

机会，时机

n. [ˌɒpəˈtjuːnəti]

考试 KET/PET/IELTS/TOEFL/PTE
科目 all

Soon he had an opportunity of explaining that to her.
不久他便有了向她解释那件事的机会。

oppose

反对；反抗

vt. [ə'pəʊz]

考试 KET/PET/IELTS/TOEFL/PTE
科目 all

He is strongly opposed to the plan.
他强烈反对这项计划。

opposite

对面的，相反的；对立的

adj. ['ɒpəzɪt]

考试 KET/PET/IELTS/TOEFL/PTE
科目 all

We lived on opposite sides of the street.
我们分别住在大街的两侧。

在……对面

prep. ['ɒpəzɪt]

考试 KET/PET/IELTS/TOEFL/PTE
科目 all

Jennie had sat opposite her at breakfast.
吃早餐时，珍妮已坐在她的对面。

opposition

敌对；反抗；反对

n. [ˌɒpə'zɪʃn]

考试 KET/PET/IELTS/TOEFL/PTE
科目 all

Much of the opposition to this plan has come from the media.
该计划的主要反对声音来自媒体。

option

选择（权）

n. ['ɒpʃn]

考试 KET/PET/IELTS/TOEFL/PTE
科目 all

The option for peace should never be closed off.
和平的选择之门永远不应被关死。

order

命令；顺序，次序；秩序；整齐；订单；等级

n. [ˈɔːdə(r)]

考试 KET/PET/IELTS/TOEFL/PTE
科目 all

The police are trying to restore public order.
警察正在努力恢复公共秩序。

订货，订购；命令；点（酒菜等）；组织，安排

v. [ˈɔːdə(r)]

考试 KET/PET/IELTS/TOEFL/PTE
科目 all

She ordered a strawberry ice-cream.
她要了一份草莓冰淇淋。

organise

组织；安排；组建；管理

v. [ˈɔːgənaɪz]

考试 KET/PET/IELTS/TOEFL/PTE
科目 all

The students organised a field trip.
学生们组织了一次实地考察旅行。

origin

起源，由来；出身，来历

n. [ˈɒrɪdʒɪn]

O

考试 KET/PET/IELTS/TOEFL/PTE
科目 all

It has been difficult to ascertain the correct source of origin.
要核实材料的正确起源很困难。

original

最初的；新颖的；有独创性的；原作的

adj. [əˈrɪdʒənl]

考试 KET/PET/IELTS/TOEFL/PTE
科目 all

I'm sticking with my original idea.
我坚持我原来的主张。

起源；原件，原稿

n. ［ə'rɪdʒənl］

考试 KET/PET/IELTS/TOEFL/
PTE
科目 all

Send out the photocopies and keep the original.
寄出复印本，保留原件。

outdoor

室外的，户外的

adj. ［'aʊtdɔ:(r)］

考试 KET/PET/IELTS/TOEFL/
PTE
科目 all

Outdoor sunlight is very good for our health.
户外的阳光对我们的健康很有好处。

outdoors

在户外，在野外

adv. ［ˌaʊt'dɔ:z］

考试 KET/PET/IELTS/TOEFL/
PTE
科目 all

The seeds may be sown outdoors in the spring.
这些种子可在春天种在户外。

outer

外部的，外面的，外层的

adj. ［'aʊtə(r)］

考试 KET/PET/IELTS/TOEFL/
PTE
科目 all

He heard a voice in the outer room.
他听到外屋有人说话。

outlook

景色，风光；展望，前景；观点，见解，人生观

n. ［'aʊtlʊk］

考试 TOEFL/IELTS/PTE
科目 reading

I adopted a positive outlook on life.
我持有积极向上的人生观。

outset

开端，开始

n. [ˈautset]

考试 KET/PET/IELTS/TOEFL/PTE
科目 all

This useless project was doomed to fail from the very outset.

这项无用的计划在最初时就注定会失败。

oven

烤炉，烤箱

n. [ˈʌvn]

考试 KET/PET/IELTS/TOEFL/PTE
科目 all

We cooked the fish in the oven.

我们在烤箱里烤鱼。

overall

包括一切的，全部的，全面的

adj. [ˌəʊvərˈɔːl]

考试 TOEFL/IELTS/PTE
科目 reading

An overall plan must be worked out.

必须制订一项全面的计划。

overhear

无意中听到，偷听到

vt. [ˌəʊvəˈhɪə(r)]

考试 TOEFL/IELTS
科目 writing

We talked quietly so as not to be overheard.

我们低声交谈，以免别人听到。

overseas

外国的，海外的

adj. [ˌəʊvəˈsiːz]

考试 KET/PET/IELTS/TOEFL/PTE
科目 all

He returned to South Africa from his long overseas trip.

他结束漫长的海外旅行回到了南非。

O

225

在海外

adv. [ˌəʊvəˈsiːz]

考试 KET/PET/IELTS/TOEFL/
PTE
科目 all

The product is sold both at home and overseas.
这个产品行销国内外。

overtime

加班；加时，延长时间；加班费

n. [ˈəʊvətaɪm]

考试 TOEFL/IELTS/PTE
科目 reading

He would work overtime, without pay, to finish a job.
他会无偿地加班把一件工作完成。

P

package

包裹；箱；标准部件；成套设备

n. [ˈpækɪdʒ]

考试 KET/PET/IELTS/TOEFL/ PTE
科目 all

He wrapped brown paper around the package.

他用棕色的纸把包裹包起来。

packaging

包装；包装工作；包装材料

n. [ˈpækɪdʒɪŋ]

考试 KET/PET/IELTS/TOEFL/ PTE
科目 all

Packaging can add several pence to the price of food.

包装会使食物的价格增加几个便士。

packing

包装；包装材料

n. [ˈpækɪŋ]

考试 KET/PET/IELTS/TOEFL/ PTE
科目 all

Packing should be strong enough to endure rough handling.

装箱应足够坚固，经得住野蛮装卸。

painful

疼痛的；令人痛苦的，令人不快的

adj. [ˈpeɪnfl]

考试 KET/PET/IELTS/TOEFL/ PTE
科目 all

A painful sickness cast a gloom over the young girl.

病痛使那个年轻的姑娘情绪低落。

paint

油漆，颜料

n. ［peɪnt］

考试 KET/PET/IELTS/TOEFL/ PTE
科目 all

They saw some large letters in white paint.
他们看见了一些用白漆写的大大的字母。

油漆；涂漆；画；描绘；描述

v. ［peɪnt］

考试 KET/PET/IELTS/TOEFL/ PTE
科目 all

I made a guitar and painted it red.
我做了一把吉他，并把它漆成了红色。

---

painting

刷油漆，着色；绘画；油画

n. ［ˈpeɪntɪŋ］

考试 KET/PET/IELTS/TOEFL/ PTE
科目 all

He shows a great aptitude in painting.
他在绘画方面表现出了很高的天赋。

---

palace

宫殿；宅邸

n. ［ˈpæləs］

考试 KET/PET/IELTS/TOEFL/ PTE
科目 all

The royal palace was filled with intrigue.
皇宫中充满了钩心斗角。

---

papercut

剪纸

n. ［ˈpeɪpəkʌt］

考试 KET/PET/IELTS/TOEFL/ PTE
科目 all

The first papercut is said to be traced back to the Northern and Southern Dynasties period.
第一幅剪纸作品据说可以追溯到南北朝时期。

parking

停放车辆

n. [ˈpɑːkɪŋ]

考试 KET/PET/IELTS/TOEFL/
PTE
科目 all

I knew I'd never find a parking space in the square.
我知道在广场上肯定找不到停车位。

partner

合伙人；伙伴；配偶

n. [ˈpɑːtnə(r)]

考试 KET/PET/IELTS/TOEFL/
PTE
科目 all

Each partner got a split of the profits.
每个合伙人得到了一份利润。

passage

通过，经过；通路，走廊；章节，段落

n. [ˈpæsɪdʒ]

考试 KET/PET/IELTS/TOEFL/
PTE
科目 all

Harry stepped into the passage and closed the door behind him.
哈里走进过道，随手关上了门。

passenger

乘客，旅客；路人

n. [ˈpæsɪndʒə(r)]

考试 KET/PET/IELTS/TOEFL/
PTE
科目 all

This is a passenger train.
这是一辆客运列车。

P

passionate

热情的，热烈的；热忱的，狂热的

adj. [ˈpæʃənət]

考试 TOEFL/IELTS/PTE
科目 reading

He is very passionate about the project.
他对那个项目非常热心。

passport

护照；手段

n. [ˈpɑːspɔːt]

考试 KET/PET/IELTS/TOEFL/PTE
科目 all

The only passport to success is hard work.
获得成功的唯一途径就是艰苦奋斗。

path

小路，小径；路线，道路；

n. [pɑːθ]

考试 KET/PET/IELTS/TOEFL/PTE
科目 all

He followed the *path* through the woods.
他沿着小路穿过了树林。

peaceful

和平的；平静的，安宁的；爱好和平的

adj. [ˈpiːsfl]

考试 KET/PET/IELTS/TOEFL/PTE
科目 all

They called for the peaceful dispersal of the demonstrators.
他们要求示威者和平解散。

peanut

花生

n. [ˈpiːnʌt]

考试 KET/PET/IELTS/TOEFL/PTE
科目 all

The soil is adaptable to the growth of peanuts.
这里的土壤适宜花生的生长。

peep

偷看，窥视

v. [piːp]

考试 TOEFL/IELTS
科目 writing

Children came to peep at him round the doorway.
孩子们围在门口偷看他。

peer

身份（或地位）相同的人；同龄人；同辈；贵族

n. [pɪə(r)]

考试 TOEFL/IELTS/PTE
科目 reading

The child is brighter than his peer.

这个孩子比他的同龄人聪明。

penetrate

穿过；透过；看穿，洞察

v. ['penətreɪt]

考试 TOEFL/IELTS
科目 writing

The nail will not penetrate.

这枚钉子钉不进去。

penny

便士；美分

n. ['peni]

考试 KET/PET/IELTS/TOEFL/
PTE
科目 all

He felt in his pocket for a penny.

他在口袋里摸索着找一个便士。

percentage

百分数，百分率，百分比

n. [pə'sentɪdʒ]

考试 KET/PET/IELTS/TOEFL/
PTE
科目 all

A high-percentage of the female staff are part-time workers.

在女职员中，兼职工作的人占很高的比例。

P

perform

履行，执行；表演，演出

v. [pə'fɔːm]

考试 KET/PET/IELTS/TOEFL/
PTE
科目 all

You should always perform what you promise.

你应该永远履行你所允诺的事。

performance

表演；绩效；执行；性能

n. ［pə'fɔːməns］

考试 KET/PET/IELTS/TOEFL/PTE
科目 all

Her performance exceeded all the others.

她的表演超过了其他所有人。

performer

执行者；表演者，演员

n. ［pə'fɔːmə(r)］

考试 KET/PET/IELTS/TOEFL/PTE
科目 all

He is a world class performer.

他是一位世界级的表演者。

perhaps

也许，大概，恐怕

adv. ［pə'hæps］

考试 KET/PET/IELTS/TOEFL/PTE
科目 all

Straighten him out; he perhaps misunderstood what I said.

向他解释清楚，他也许误解了我的意思。

permission

允许，同意

n. ［pə'mɪʃn］

考试 KET/PET/IELTS/TOEFL/PTE
科目 all

No official permission has been given for the event to take place.

这项活动未得到任何批准，不能进行。

permit

许可，允许

v. ［pə'mɪt］

考试 KET/PET/IELTS/TOEFL/PTE
科目 all

Do you permit your children to smoke?

你允许你的孩子们吸烟吗？

许可证，执照

n. ［ˈpɜːmɪt］

考试 KET/PET/IELTS/TOEFL/
PTE
科目 all

I have had a working permit from the immigration office.
我已从移民局获得工作许可证。

persistence

坚持；持续，存留

n. ［pəˈsɪstəns］

考试 TOEFL/IELTS/PTE
科目 reading

I admire your persistence enormously.
我非常崇拜你的毅力。

personnel

职员，全体人员；人事部门

n. ［ˌpɜːsəˈnel］

考试 TOEFL/IELTS/PTE
科目 reading

All personnel of the company is eligible for the retirement plan.
公司所有员工都有资格参加这项退休计划。

petrol

汽油

n. ［ˈpetrəl］

P

考试 KET/PET/IELTS/TOEFL/
PTE
科目 all

I think the price of the petrol will spiral up.
我认为汽油的价格将会上涨。

petroleum

石油

n. ［pəˈtrəʊliəm］

考试 KET/PET/IELTS/TOEFL/
PTE
科目 all

Indonesia is abundant in petroleum deposits.
印度尼西亚的石油蕴藏量丰富。

phrase

短语，词组；习语，成语，警句，惯用法

n. ［freɪz］

考试 KET/PET/IELTS/TOEFL/PTE
科目 all

This bland phrase amounts to a revolution.
这一单调的短语其实意味着一场革命。

physical

物质的；身体的；物理的

adj. ［ˈfɪzɪkl］

考试 KET/PET/IELTS/TOEFL/PTE
科目 all

I have no idea how large the physical universe is.
我不知道物质世界有多大。

physicist

物理学家

n. ［ˈfɪzɪsɪst］

考试 KET/PET/IELTS/TOEFL/PTE
科目 all

He wanted to be a physicist.
他曾经希望成为一名物理学家。

physics

物理（学）

n. ［ˈfɪzɪks］

考试 KET/PET/IELTS/TOEFL/PTE
科目 all

He was awarded the Nobel Prize for Physics.
他被授予诺贝尔物理学奖。

pigeon

鸽子

n. ［ˈpɪdʒɪn］

考试 KET/PET/IELTS/TOEFL/PTE
科目 all

A pigeon perched on our porch railing.
一只鸽子停留在我们门廊的栏杆上。

pill

药丸，药片

n. ［pɪl］

考试 KET/PET/IELTS/TOEFL/
PTE
科目 all
Why do I have to take all these pills?
我为什么非得服下所有这些药丸呢?

pillow

枕头

n. ［ˈpɪləʊ］

考试 KET/PET/IELTS/TOEFL/
PTE
科目 all
I rested my head on a soft pillow filled with feathers.
我头枕着填满羽毛的柔软枕头。

pilot

飞行员；试验

n. ［ˈpaɪlət］

考试 KET/PET/IELTS/TOEFL/
PTE
科目 all
The pilot was able to land the plane safely.
这名飞行员安全地着陆了。

驾驶；试驾；试用

vt. ［ˈpaɪlət］

考试 KET/PET/IELTS/TOEFL/
PTE
科目 all
He piloted his own plane part of the way to Washington.
乘私人飞机去华盛顿的路上，有一段行程是他自己驾驶的。

pine

难过，悲伤；消瘦，虚弱

vi. ［pain］

考试 TOEFL/IELTS
科目 writing
He began to peak and pine.
他日渐消瘦。

planet

行星

n. [ˈplænɪt]

考试 KET/PET/IELTS/TOEFL/ PTE
科目 all

The earth is one of the planets in the Galaxy.
地球是银河系中的行星之一。

plastic

塑料；塑料制品

n. [ˈplæstɪk]

考试 KET/PET/IELTS/TOEFL/ PTE
科目 all

The pipes should be made of plastic.
这些管子应该用塑料制作。

塑料的，塑料制的；可塑的，有塑性的

adj. [ˈplæstɪk]

考试 KET/PET/IELTS/TOEFL/ PTE
科目 all

The mind of a young child is quite plastic.
儿童的思想很有可塑性。

plead

恳求，请求；辩护，为……辩护；提出……为理由

v. [pliːd]

考试 TOEFL/IELTS
科目 writing

His mother did her best to plead his case.
他的母亲尽力为他的案件辩护。

plunder

抢劫，掠夺

v. [ˈplʌndə(r)]

考试 TOEFL/IELTS
科目 writing

They plundered all the valuable things they could find.
他们抢劫了所有能找到的值钱东西。

pocket

衣袋，口袋，兜

n. [ˈpɒkɪt]

考试 KET/PET/IELTS/TOEFL/
PTE
科目 all

The man stood with his hands in his pockets.
那个男人双手插在兜里站着。

把……装入袋内；攫取，揩油，中饱私囊；挣，
赚下

vt. [ˈpɒkɪt]

考试 KET/PET/IELTS/TOEFL/
PTE
科目 all

Dishonest importers would be able to pocket the VAT collected from customers.
不诚实的进口商将能够把从顾客那里收取的增值税据
为己有。

poet

诗人

n. [ˈpəʊɪt]

考试 KET/PET/IELTS/TOEFL/
PTE
科目 all

He dreamed of becoming a poet.
他梦想成为一位诗人。

poetry

诗歌，诗集

n. [ˈpəʊətri]

考试 KET/PET/IELTS/TOEFL/
PTE
科目 all

Do you know the chief distinction of Chinese poetry?
你知道中国诗歌的主要特征吗？

P

polar

两极的；极地的；南辕北辙的，完全相反的

adj. [ˈpəʊlə(r)]

考试 KET/PET/IELTS/TOEFL/
PTE
科目 all

Are there any animals in the polar circles?
南极圈和北极圈内有动物存在吗？

policy

政策；保险单

n. [ˈpɒləsi]

考试 KET/PET/IELTS/TOEFL/PTE
科目 all

Concern for the environment is at the core of our policy.

对环境的关注是我们政策的核心。

pollute

弄脏，污染

vt. [pəˈluːt]

考试 KET/PET/IELTS/TOEFL/PTE
科目 all

Cars not only pollute the air in cities, but make them crowded.

汽车不仅污染城市空气，而且使城市拥挤不堪。

pollution

污染

n. [pəˈluːʃn]

考试 KET/PET/IELTS/TOEFL/PTE
科目 all

We have freed the lake from pollution.

我们已经清除了该湖的污染。

pond

池塘

n. [pɒnd]

考试 KET/PET/IELTS/TOEFL/PTE
科目 all

The children are splashing in the pond.

孩子们在池塘里戏水。

ponder

深思，考虑

v. [ˈpɒndə(r)]

考试 TOEFL/IELTS
科目 writing

He wanted to ponder the next move.

他想考虑一下下一步怎么办。

port

港口；舱门，舱口；(船、飞机等的) 左舷

n. [pɔːt]

考试 KET/PET/IELTS/TOEFL/PTE
科目 all

They all boarded the ship before it left the port.

在船离开港口前，他们都登上了船。

portray

描写，描述

vt. [pɔːˈtreɪ]

考试 TOEFL/IELTS
科目 writing

The father is portrayed as a coward in this play.

父亲在这部戏剧里被描写成一个懦弱的人。

position

位置；职位；姿势，姿态；见解

n. [pəˈzɪʃn]

考试 KET/PET/IELTS/TOEFL/PTE
科目 all

Make sure that you are working in a comfortable position.

工作时一定要保持舒适的姿势。

positive

确定的，明确的；自信的；积极的，建设性的

adj. [ˈpɒzətɪv]

考试 KET/PET/IELTS/TOEFL/PTE
科目 all

There are positive changes that should be implemented in the rearing of animals.

应该对动物饲养进行明确的改革。

P

postpone

推迟，延缓

vt. [pəˈspəʊn]

考试 TOEFL/IELTS
科目 writing

Could we postpone our meeting to sometime early next week?

我们能否将会议推迟到下星期的前面几天？

powerful

强大的，强有力的，有权势的

adj. ['paʊəfl]

考试 TOEFL/IELTS/PTE
科目 reading

You're a powerful man — people will listen to you.
你是个有影响力的人，大家会听你的。

practical

实际的；可行的；实用的

adj. ['præktɪkl]

考试 KET/PET/IELTS/TOEFL/PTE
科目 all

He dealt with practical military developments.
他谈到了军事发展的实际情况。

praise

赞扬，歌颂；表扬

vt. [preɪz]

考试 KET/PET/IELTS/TOEFL/PTE
科目 all

He praised the excellent work of the UN weapons inspectors.
他赞扬了联合国武器核查人员的出色工作。

称赞，赞美；赞美的话

n. [preɪz]

考试 KET/PET/IELTS/TOEFL/PTE
科目 all

That is high praise indeed.
那真是高度的赞美。

predict

预言，预测，预告

vt. [prɪ'dɪkt]

考试 KET/PET/IELTS/TOEFL/PTE
科目 all

You can never predict what would happen next.
谁也无法预料接下来会发生什么事。

preference

偏爱，喜爱；优先选择

n. ['prefrəns]

考试 KET/PET/IELTS/TOEFL/
PTE
科目 all

It's a matter of personal preference.

那是个人的爱好问题。

---

premises

建筑物，房屋；营业场所

n. ['premɪsɪz]

考试 TOEFL/IELTS/PTE
科目 reading

No alcohol may be consumed on the premises.

场区内禁止饮酒。

---

prepare

准备，预备

v. [prɪ'peə(r)]

考试 KET/PET/IELTS/TOEFL/
PTE
科目 all

We must prepare the room for the meeting.

我们必须为会议准备好房间。

---

prepared

准备好的；愿意的；期望的

adj. [prɪ'peəd]

考试 KET/PET/IELTS/TOEFL/
PTE
科目 all

She was not prepared for the bad news.

她对这则坏消息没有思想准备。

---

pressing

急迫的；再三要求的，恳切要求的

adj. ['presɪŋ]

考试 TOEFL/IELTS/PTE
科目 reading

This is the most pressing task at present.

这是当前最急迫的任务。

P

presume

假定，假设；认为；滥用，擅自行动

v. [prɪˈzjuːm]

考试 TOEFL/IELTS
科目 writing

I presume legislators expect the president to save them.

我推测，立法者希望总统拯救他们。

pretend

假装，假托；自称，自认为；装扮，扮作

v. [prɪˈtend]

考试 KET/PET/IELTS/TOEFL/PTE
科目 all

You pretend to be foolish intentionally.

你有意装傻。

prevail

流行，盛行；战胜

vi. [prɪˈveɪl]

考试 TOEFL/IELTS/PTE
科目 reading

This old custom does not prevail now.

这种旧风俗现在已经不流行了。

primary

最初的，初级的；首要的，主要的，基本的

adj. [ˈpraɪməri]

考试 KET/PET/IELTS/TOEFL/PTE
科目 all

China is currently in the primary stage of socialism.

中国正处于社会主义初级阶段。

printer

打印机；印刷工人；印刷厂

n. [ˈprɪntə(r)]

考试 KET/PET/IELTS/TOEFL/PTE
科目 all

I want to buy a printer.

我要买一台打印机。

private

私人的，个人的；秘密的，私下的

adj. [ˈpraɪvət]

考试 KET/PET/IELTS/TOEFL/ PTE
科目 all

The king invaded our private rights.

国王侵犯了我们个人的权利。

二等兵，列兵

n. [ˈpraɪvət]

考试 KET/PET/IELTS/TOEFL/ PTE
科目 all

He was broken from sergeant to private.

他从中士降为列兵。

privilege

特权；优惠待遇

n. [ˈprɪvəlɪdʒ]

考试 TOEFL/IELTS/PTE
科目 reading

We need to allow a privilege to him.

我们需要给他一种特权。

prize

奖赏；奖金；奖品

n. [praɪz]

考试 KET/PET/IELTS/TOEFL/ PTE
科目 all

He was awarded the Nobel Prize for Physics in 1985.

他于 1985 年被授予诺贝尔物理学奖。

珍视，珍惜

vt. [praɪz]

考试 KET/PET/IELTS/TOEFL/ PTE
科目 all

Military figures made out of lead are prized by collectors.

收藏家们对铅铸的军人塑像视若珍宝。

P

probable

很可能的

adj. [ˈprɒbəbl]

考试 KET/PET/IELTS/TOEFL/PTE
科目 all

It is probable that the medication will suppress the symptom without treating the condition.
这种药物有可能治标不治本。

procure

取得；获得

v. [prəˈkjʊə(r)]

考试 TOEFL/IELTS
科目 writing

It remained very difficult to procure food, fuel and other daily necessities.
食物、燃料和其他日用必需品仍然很难得到。

profess

表白；声称，宣称

vt. [prəˈfes]

考试 TOEFL/IELTS
科目 writing

I don't profess to be an expert in that subject.
我并没有声称自己是那方面的专家。

profession

职业，专业；表白；宣布

n. [prəˈfeʃn]

考试 KET/PET/IELTS/TOEFL/PTE
科目 all

Have you ever thought about a career in the medical profession?
你考虑过从事医疗职业吗？

professional

职业的，专业的

adj. [prəˈfeʃənl]

考试 KET/PET/IELTS/TOEFL/PTE
科目 all

A lawyer is a professional man.
律师是从事专门职业的人。

专业人员

n. [prəˈfeʃənl]

考试 KET/PET/IELTS/TOEFL/
PTE
科目 all

My father wanted me to become a professional and have more stability.

我父亲想让我成为专业人士，这样能更稳定一些。

proficient

熟练的，精通的

adj. [prəˈfɪʃnt]

考试 TOEFL/IELTS/PTE
科目 reading

A great number of Egyptians are proficient in foreign languages.

很多埃及人都精通外语。

prolong

延长；拖延

vt. [prəˈlɒŋ]

考试 TOEFL/IELTS/PTE
科目 reading

How can we endeavour to prolong the brevity of human life?

我们怎样才能延长短暂的人生？

promise

诺言；指望；前途；迹象

n. [ˈprɒmɪs]

考试 KET/PET/IELTS/TOEFL/
PTE
科目 all

If you make a promise, you should keep it.

如果你许下一个诺言，你就应该遵守它。

P

许诺；有指望；有前途；预示

v. [ˈprɒmɪs]

考试 KET/PET/IELTS/TOEFL/
PTE
科目 all

Promise me you will not waste your time.

答应我，不要浪费自己的时间。

promotion

促进；提升；创立

n. ['prə'məʊʃn]

考试 TOEFL/IELTS/PTE
科目 reading

It was great to hear about your recent promotion.
听说你最近得到了提升，这好极了。

propagate

繁殖，增殖；传播；宣传

v. ['prɒpəgeɪt]

考试 TOEFL/IELTS
科目 writing

The weeds propagate themselves rapidly.
杂草繁殖极快。

proposal

提议，建议；求婚

n. [prə'pəʊzl]

考试 TOEFL/IELTS/PTE
科目 reading

His proposal that the system should be changed was rejected.
他提出的关于修改制度的建议被拒绝了。

prosecute

起诉，告发；实行，从事

v. ['prɒsɪkjuːt]

考试 TOEFL/IELTS
科目 writing

He is being prosecuted for two criminal offences.
他因两项刑事罪名被起诉。

prospect

景色；前景；可能性，希望

n. ['prɒspekt]

考试 TOEFL/IELTS/PTE
科目 reading

I chose to work abroad to improve my career prospects.
我选择出国工作以求在事业上有更好的发展。

provide

供应，提供；规定；预备，防备

v. [prə'vaɪd]

考试 KET/PET/IELTS/TOEFL/PTE
科目 all

The government was not in a position to provide them with food.

政府不可能给他们提供食物。

province

省；领域，范围

n. ['prɒvɪns]

考试 KET/PET/IELTS/TOEFL/PTE
科目 all

Most of the province is as flat as a pancake.

那个省的大部分地区地势平坦。

psychological

心理的，心理学的

adj. [ˌsaɪkə'lɒdʒɪkl]

考试 TOEFL/IELTS/PTE
科目 reading

He was adept at maintaining a psychological advantage.

他善于保持一种心理上的优势。

publication

出版物；出版，发表

n. [ˌpʌblɪ'keɪʃn]

考试 KET/PET/IELTS/TOEFL/PTE
科目 all

These volumes are an official publication of the Court.

这套书是联邦最高法院的官方出版物。

P

pumpkin

南瓜，南瓜大果

n. ['pʌmpkɪn]

考试 KET/PET/IELTS/TOEFL/PTE
科目 all

The pumpkin is a real monster.

这个南瓜可真大。

punishment

惩罚，处罚

n. [ˈpʌnɪʃmənt]

考试 KET/PET/IELTS/TOEFL/PTE
科目 all

Luckily, he escaped from punishment.
侥幸得很，他没有受到处罚。

purchase

购买，采购

n. [ˈpɜːtʃəs]

考试 TOEFL/IELTS/PTE
科目 reading

He gave his son some money for the purchase of his school books.
他给儿子一些钱购买学校的课本。

purple

紫色

n. [ˈpɜːpl]

考试 KET/PET/IELTS/TOEFL/PTE
科目 all

She wore purple and green silk.
她穿着紫绿相间的绸缎衣服。

pursue

追赶，追踪；继续，从事

vt. [pəˈsjuː]

考试 TOEFL/IELTS
科目 writing

She pushed herself to pursue a musical career.
她发奋努力去追求音乐生涯。

puzzle

难题；谜

n. [ˈpʌzl]

考试 KET/PET/IELTS/TOEFL/PTE
科目 all

I'm doing a word puzzle in this newspaper.
我正在玩这张报纸上的猜字谜游戏。

迷惑，使困惑

vt. [ˈpʌzl]

考试 KET/PET/IELTS/TOEFL/PTE
科目 all

My sister puzzles me and causes me anxiety.
我妹妹总让我捉摸不透，弄得我焦虑不安。

Q

quality

质量，品质；特性；才能

n. ['kwɒləti]

考试 KET/PET/IELTS/TOEFL/PTE
科目 all

When costs are cut product quality suffers.
一降低成本，产品质量就会受到影响。

queue

行列，队；队列

n. [kjuː]

考试 KET/PET/IELTS/TOEFL/PTE
科目 all

At the head of the queue was an old woman.
在队列的前面有一个老妇人。

（使）排队，排队等待

v. [kjuː]

考试 KET/PET/IELTS/TOEFL/PTE
科目 all

I had to queue for quite a while.
我不得不排一会儿队。

quiver

颤动，振动

vi. ['kwɪvə(r)]

考试 TOEFL/IELTS
科目 writing

He quivered all over with rage.
他气得浑身发抖。

R

radiate

辐射，发出（光或热）；显示，流露；传播

v. [ˈreɪdieɪt]

考试 TOEFL/IELTS
科目 writing

From here, contaminated air radiates out to the open countryside.
被污染的空气从这里扩散到开阔的乡村地区。

rag

破布，碎布

n. [ræg]

考试 KET/PET/IELTS/TOEFL/PTE
科目 all

The highest quality paper is made mostly from rags.
上好的纸多半是用破布制造的。

raise

举起；增加；饲养；引起

vt. [reɪz]

考试 KET/PET/IELTS/TOEFL/PTE
科目 all

If you know the answer, please raise your hand up.
如果你知道答案，请举起手。

ramble

漫步，闲逛；漫谈

n. [ˈræmbl]

考试 TOEFL/IELTS
科目 writing

An hour's ramble through the woods is good for you.
一个小时的林间漫步对你有好处。

rank

地位，级别；军衔；行列；等级

n. ［ræŋk］

考试 KET/PET/IELTS/TOEFL/ PTE
科目 all

They are people of all ranks and classes.
他们来自各阶层各阶级。

分等级，把……分类；属于某等级

v. ［ræŋk］

考试 KET/PET/IELTS/TOEFL/ PTE
科目 all

We rank him among the best tennis players.
我们把他列入最优秀网球运动员之列。

rapid

急速的；险峻的

adj. ［'ræpɪd］

考试 KET/PET/IELTS/TOEFL/ PTE
科目 all

He walked at a rapid pace along Charles Street.
他快步走过查尔斯大街。

(*pl.*) 急流，湍急的河水

n. ［'ræpɪd］

考试 KET/PET/IELTS/TOEFL/ PTE
科目 all

They fell into the seething waters of the rapids.
他们跌进了汹涌的急流中。

rather

相当；相反，反而，而是

adv. ［'rɑːðə(r)］

考试 KET/PET/IELTS/TOEFL/ PTE
科目 all

My finances are rather wobbly.
我的财务状况相当不稳定。

R

ratify

批准，认可

vt. [ˈrætɪfaɪ]

考试 TOEFL/IELTS
科目 writing

The heads of two governments met to ratify the peace treaty.

两国政府首脑会晤批准和平条约。

rational

理性的，合理的；理智的，清醒的

adj. [ˈræʃnəl]

考试 TOEFL/IELTS/PTE
科目 reading

There is no rational explanation for his actions.

对他的所作所为无法给出合理的解释。

realism

现实主义，现实性

n. [ˈriːəlɪzəm]

考试 KET/PET/IELTS/TOEFL/PTE
科目 all

The early ambitions of youthful enthusiasm soon become tempered with realism.

之前年少时对理想抱负怀有的一腔热情很快便被现实浇灭。

realistic

现实（主义）的；逼真的

adj. [ˌriːəˈlɪstɪk]

考试 KET/PET/IELTS/TOEFL/PTE
科目 all

We have to be realistic about our chances of winning.

我们必须实事求是地估计我们获胜的可能性。

realize

认识到；体会到；实现

v. [ˈriːəlaɪz]

考试 KET/PET/IELTS/TOEFL/PTE
科目 all

You must realize that it is arrogance that has cramped your progress.

你应该认识到是骄傲阻碍了你的进步。

reap

收割，收获；获得，得到

v. [riːp]

考试 TOEFL/IELTS
科目 writing

They are reaping a field of wheat.
他们正在收割一片麦田。

reasonable

明智的；合理的；公平的

adj. ['riːznəbl]

考试 TOEFL/IELTS/PTE
科目 reading

Such fears are reasonable, but often exaggerated.
这样的担忧在情理之中，但往往言过其实。

recall

召回；回忆；使想起

v. [rɪˈkɔːl]

考试 KET/PET/IELTS/TOEFL/
PTE
科目 all

I can't recall how to do it.
我回忆不起该怎么做了。

召回；撤销

n. [rɪˈkɔːl]

考试 KET/PET/IELTS/TOEFL/
PTE
科目 all

He had a good memory, and total recall of her spoken words.
他有好记性，能完全回忆起她说过的话。

R

recede

后退；撤回；减弱

vi. [rɪˈsiːd]

考试 TOEFL/IELTS
科目 writing

As the tide receded we were able to look for shells.
潮水退去后，我们就能寻找贝壳了。

recipe

食谱，配方

n. [ˈresəpi]

考试 KET/PET/IELTS/TOEFL/PTE
科目 all

In the recipe, it says that I must use two eggs.
这个食谱上说我必须用两个鸡蛋。

recite

背诵；列举

v. [rɪˈsaɪt]

考试 KET/PET/IELTS/TOEFL/PTE
科目 all

He is going to recite a poem.
他将要朗诵一首诗。

recognition

认出；辨认；承认；重视；赏识

n. [ˌrekəgˈnɪʃn]

考试 TOEFL/IELTS/PTE
科目 reading

My recognition of him was immediate.
我一见就认出是他。

recompense

回报，酬谢

vt. [ˈrekəmpens]

考试 TOEFL/IELTS
科目 writing

If they succeed in court, they will be fully recompensed for their loss.
如果他们能在法庭上胜诉，他们的损失将会得到全额赔偿。

recorder

记录员；录音机

n. [rɪˈkɔːdə(r)]

考试 KET/PET/IELTS/TOEFL/PTE
科目 all

The recorder is different in colour from that of the original sample.
录音机的颜色不同于样品的颜色。

recruit

招募；吸收；补充

v. [rɪˈkruːt]

考试 TOEFL/IELTS/PTE
科目 reading

Can't you recruit more members to the music society?

你不能再吸收一些人加入音乐协会吗？

redound

增加，促进，有助于

vi. [riˈdaʊnd]

考试 TOEFL/IELTS
科目 writing

My skill in such matters might redound to my advantage.

我在这些事情上的技能可能会对我有所帮助。

reef

礁石，暗礁

n. [riːf]

考试 KET/PET/IELTS/TOEFL/PTE
科目 all

But a changing environment could put the reef's future in jeopardy.

但不断变化的环境也许会让珊瑚礁的未来处于危险之中。

reference

证明；参照；涉及；提及

n. [ˈrefrəns]

考试 TOEFL/IELTS/PTE
科目 reading

Please keep this sheet in a safe place for reference.

请把这张纸放在稳妥之处以备查阅。

reform

改革，革新；重组；（使）改正

v. [rɪˈfɔːm]

考试 TOEFL/IELTS/PTE
科目 reading

The leader thinks the only solution is to reform his party.

领导者认为唯一的解决方法是改革政党内部。

R

refuse

拒绝，谢绝

v. [rɪˈfjuːz]

考试 KET/PET/IELTS/TOEFL/PTE
科目 all

He refused my offer of help.

他拒绝了我的帮助。

废物，垃圾

n. [ˈrefjuːs]

考试 KET/PET/IELTS/TOEFL/PTE
科目 all

The District Council made a weekly collection of refuse.

区政务委员会每周收集一次垃圾。

regard

把……看作；看待；注视

vt. [rɪˈɡɑːd]

考试 KET/PET/IELTS/TOEFL/PTE
科目 all

I regard creativity both as a gift and as a skill.

我认为创造力既是一种天赋也是一种技巧。

敬重；问候

n. [rɪˈɡɑːd]

考试 KET/PET/IELTS/TOEFL/PTE
科目 all

I have a very high regard for him and what he has achieved.

我非常钦佩他的为人和成就。

regret

后悔，惋惜；抱歉

v. [rɪˈɡret]

考试 KET/PET/IELTS/TOEFL/PTE
科目 all

We regret to inform you that your application has not been successful.

我们很遗憾地通知您，您的申请未通过。

遗憾，抱歉，懊悔

n. ［rɪˈgret］

考试 KET/PET/IELTS/TOEFL/PTE
科目 all

Lillee said he had no regrets about retiring.
利里说他不后悔退休。

regretful

遗憾的，后悔的，惋惜的

adj. ［rɪˈgretfl］

考试 KET/PET/IELTS/TOEFL/PTE
科目 all

Surprisingly, she didn't feel nervous, or regretful about her actions.
令人惊讶的是，她并没有对她的行为感到紧张或后悔。

regular

有规律的；整齐的，匀称的；正规的

adj. ［ˈregjələ(r)］

考试 KET/PET/IELTS/TOEFL/PTE
科目 all

We're going to be meeting there on a regular basis.
我们将定期在那里会面。

rehearse

排练，排演；背诵，默默地练习

v. ［riˈhɜːs］

考试 TOEFL/IELTS
科目 writing

The cast and crew were only given three and a half weeks to rehearse.
演员和剧组工作人员只有三周半的时间进行排练。

R

rejoice

欣喜，高兴

v. ［rɪˈdʒɔɪs］

考试 TOEFL/IELTS
科目 writing

I rejoice that you have recovered so quickly.
听到你已很快痊愈，我很高兴。

relate

叙述，讲述；使互相关联

v. [rɪˈleɪt]

考试 TOEFL/IELTS/PTE
科目 reading

It is difficult to relate cause and effect in this case.

这个案件中的动机与结果很难联系起来。

related

与……有关的；相关的

adj. [rɪˈleɪtɪd]

考试 KET/PET/IELTS/TOEFL/
PTE
科目 all

People should know the related regulations before they exploit natural resources.

在开发自然资源前，人们应该先了解相关的规定。

relation

关系，联系；亲属，亲戚

n. [rɪˈleɪʃn]

考试 KET/PET/IELTS/TOEFL/
PTE
科目 all

We try to maintain good relation with our customers.

我们努力与客户保持良好的关系。

relaxation

放松，松弛

n. [ˌriːlækˈseɪʃn]

考试 KET/PET/IELTS/TOEFL/
PTE
科目 all

Relaxation exercises can free your body of tension.

放松运动可以舒缓身体的紧张。

reliable

可靠的，可信赖的

adj. [rɪˈlaɪəbl]

考试 TOEFL/IELTS/PTE
科目 reading

I don't think he is a reliable man.

我认为他不是一个可靠的人。

reluctant

不愿的，勉强的

adj. [rɪˈlʌktənt]

考试 TOEFL/IELTS/PTE
科目 reading

He gave me a reluctant assistance.

他很不情愿地帮了我。

remembrance

回忆，记忆；纪念品

n. [rɪˈmembrəns]

考试 KET/PET/IELTS/TOEFL/
PTE
科目 all

Let us mark this day with remembrance, of who we are and how far we have travelled.

让我们以怀念纪念这个日子，回想我们是谁，我们走了多远。

remit

汇款，汇出；免除

vt. [rɪˈmɪt]

考试 TOEFL/IELTS
科目 writing

Many immigrants regularly remit money to their families.

许多移民定期给他们的家人汇款。

render

提供；报答；翻译；给予补偿

vt. [ˈrendə(r)]

考试 TOEFL/IELTS
科目 writing

Any assistance you can render him will be appreciated.

无论给予何种帮助，他都会非常感激。

R

rental

租借的；租金的

adj. [ˈrentl]

考试 KET/PET/IELTS/TOEFL/
PTE
科目 all

Repairs and improvements can lead to higher rental rates.

修缮后可以提高租价。

repair

修理，修补

n. [rɪˈpeə(r)]

考试 KET/PET/IELTS/TOEFL/PTE
科目 all

The dome of the church is under repair.
教堂的圆顶在修。

补救，纠正；修理

vt. [rɪˈpeə(r)]

考试 KET/PET/IELTS/TOEFL/PTE
科目 all

It must be repaired by a qualified worker.
这个应由专业人员来维修。

reporter

通讯员，记者

n. [rɪˈpɔːtə(r)]

考试 KET/PET/IELTS/TOEFL/PTE
科目 all

I preferred the title of reporter.
我更喜欢记者这个头衔。

represent

代表；相当于，意味着；体现；展示

vt. [ˌreprɪˈzent]

考试 KET/PET/IELTS/TOEFL/PTE
科目 all

They represent all social strata.
他们代表各个社会阶层。

reputation

名誉，名声

n. [ˌrepjuˈteɪʃn]

考试 TOEFL/IELTS/PTE
科目 reading

He has a reputation for being courageous in his hometown.
他在家乡以勇敢闻名。

request

要求，请求

n. [rɪˈkwest]

考试 KET/PET/IELTS/TOEFL/PTE
科目 all

France had agreed to his request for political asylum.

法国已经同意了他寻求政治庇护的请求。

要求，请求

vt. [rɪˈkwest]

考试 KET/PET/IELTS/TOEFL/PTE
科目 all

She had requested that the door to her room be left open.

她请求不要关闭通向她房间的门。

---

require

需要；要求；命令

vt. [rɪˈkwaɪə(r)]

考试 KET/PET/IELTS/TOEFL/PTE
科目 all

If you require further information, you should consult the registrar.

如果需要进一步了解信息，请咨询教务主任。

---

resist

抵抗，反抗；忍得住；抵制

v. [rɪˈzɪst]

考试 TOEFL/IELTS/PTE
科目 reading

Some substances resist corrosion by air or water.

有些物质可以抵抗空气或水的腐蚀。

---

resolution

决议；分辨率；解决；分解

n. [ˌrezəˈluːʃn]

考试 KET/PET/IELTS/TOEFL/PTE
科目 all

The house resolution would slash support for international family planning and reproductive health care.

众议院的决定会影响国际计划生育和生育医疗保健的资助。

R

resource

资源；机智；财力；谋略

n. [rɪˈsɔːs]

考试 KET/PET/IELTS/TOEFL/
PTE
科目 all

The government should take steps to preserve the natural resource.

政府应该采取一定的措施保护自然资源。

respect

尊敬，尊重

vt. [rɪˈspekt]

考试 KET/PET/IELTS/TOEFL/
PTE
科目 all

His accomplishments earned respect for him.

他的成就赢得了人们的尊敬。

敬意；问候；关系；方面

n. [rɪˈspekt]

考试 KET/PET/IELTS/TOEFL/
PTE
科目 all

His voice was warm with friendship and respect.

他温和的声音里充满了友善和敬意。

restaurant

餐馆，饭店

n. [ˈrestrɒnt]

考试 KET/PET/IELTS/TOEFL/
PTE
科目 all

We're going to the Japanese restaurant.

我们要去那家日本料理餐厅。

restock

重新进货，再储存

v. [ˌriːˈstɒk]

考试 TOEFL/IELTS
科目 writing

In Germany, consumers used the period of low prices to restock heating oil, providing a boost to demand.

在德国，消费者利用低油价期重新储备取暖油，这提振了需求。

resume

重新开始；继续；重新占用

v. [rɪ'zjuːm]

考试 TOEFL/IELTS/PTE
科目 reading

The two sides will resume negotiations with radically different expectations.

双方也将带着根本不同的期望继续协商。

retail

零售

n. ['riːteɪl]

考试 TOEFL/IELTS/PTE
科目 reading

The recommended retail price is £9.99.

建议零售价为 9.99 英镑。

retire

退休，引退；退出，撤退；就寝

v. [rɪ'taɪə(r)]

考试 KET/PET/IELTS/TOEFL/PTE
科目 all

Many people worry about their finances when they retire.

很多人担心自己退休之后的经济状况。

retort

反驳，反击

vt. [rɪ'tɔːt]

考试 TOEFL/IELTS
科目 writing

Sam retorted that it was my fault as much as his.

山姆反驳说我和他同样有错。

R

reveal

展现，显示；揭示，揭露；告诉；泄露

vt. [rɪ'viːl]

考试 KET/PET/IELTS/TOEFL/PTE
科目 all

Surveys revealed a collapse in consumer confidence last winter.

调查显示去年冬天消费者的信心急剧下降了。

revert

回复；重提

vi. [rɪˈvɜːt]

考试 TOEFL/IELTS
科目 writing

His manner seems to have reverted to normal.
他的举止好像已经恢复了正常。

review

回顾；检查；评论

vt. [rɪˈvjuː]

考试 KET/PET/IELTS/TOEFL/
PTE
科目 all

She expects it will take about four days to review all the material.
她预计将要花费四天时间对全部素材进行复审。

回顾；检查；评论

n. [rɪˈvjuː]

考试 KET/PET/IELTS/TOEFL/
PTE
科目 all

We've never had a good review in the music press.
我们从未在音乐媒体获得过好评。

revive

苏醒，复活；复兴，再流行

v. [rɪˈvaɪv]

考试 TOEFL/IELTS
科目 writing

His encouraging words revived my drooping spirits.
他令人鼓舞的话使我颓丧的精神振作起来。

revoke

废除；取消；撤回

vt. [rɪˈvəʊk]

考试 TOEFL/IELTS
科目 writing

The government revoked her husband's licence to operate migrant labour crews.
政府撤销了她丈夫管理外来打工人群的许可证。

revolve

使旋转，使绕转

vi. [rɪˈvɒlv]

考试 TOEFL/IELTS
科目 writing

The earth revolves on its axis.

地球环绕自身的轴心转动。

reward

奖赏，报酬

n. [rɪˈwɔːd]

考试 TOEFL/IELTS/PTE
科目 reading

He was given the job as a reward for running a successful leadership bid.

因为成功组织了领导职位竞选活动，他得到了这份工作。

rigid

僵硬的；不弯曲的；严格的

adj. [ˈrɪdʒɪd]

考试 TOEFL/IELTS/PTE
科目 reading

The company has a rigid network censorship program.

这家公司有着严格的网络监控程序。

root

根，根部；根本；根源

n. [ruːt]

考试 KET/PET/IELTS/TOEFL/PTE
科目 all

Money，or love of money，is said to be the root of all evil.

有人说钱和爱钱是万恶之源。

(使）生根；（使）扎根

v. [ruːt]

考试 KET/PET/IELTS/TOEFL/PTE
科目 all

Most plants will root in about six to eight weeks.

大多数植物都会在六到八周内生根。

R

rope

绳，索

n. ［rəʊp］

考试 KET/PET/IELTS/TOEFL/PTE
科目 all

They waited for the crew chief to give the signal to throw the rope.

他们等待着乘务长发出抛下绳索的信号。

rot

腐烂

v. ［rɒt］

考试 TOEFL/IELTS
科目 writing

The window frame had rotted away completely.

窗框已经完全烂掉了。

rouse

唤醒，唤起；激励；激起

vt. ［raʊz］

考试 TOEFL/IELTS
科目 writing

The clock roused me from my sleep at 6 a. m.

早晨 6 点钟，电话铃声就把我从睡梦中吵醒了。

routine

例行公事，惯例，常规

n. ［ruːˈtiːn］

考试 TOEFL/IELTS/PTE
科目 reading

We clean and repair the machines as a matter of routine.

我们定期清洗和修理机器。

rubber

橡皮，橡胶；橡胶制品；胶鞋

n. ［ˈrʌbə(r)］

考试 KET/PET/IELTS/TOEFL/PTE
科目 all

Natural rubber has been gathered from the sap of plants for centuries.

从植物汁液中收集天然橡胶已经有几个世纪的历史。

rude

粗鲁的；猛烈的，残暴的；粗糙的，粗陋的

adj. [ruːd]

考试 KET/PET/IELTS/TOEFL/PTE
科目 all

Unfair bosses and rude customers make us unhappy on the job.

不公正的老板和粗鲁的顾客让我们工作起来很不愉快。

rug

小地毯；厚毯子

n. [rʌg]

考试 KET/PET/IELTS/TOEFL/PTE
科目 all

The old lady was seated in her chair at the window, a rug over her knees.

老太太坐在窗边的椅子上，膝盖上盖着一条毯子。

rural

农村的

adj. ['rʊərəl]

考试 KET/PET/IELTS/TOEFL/PTE
科目 all

Little bridges, murmuring brooks and rural cottages, all of these come into a picture of quietness and simplicity.

小桥、潺潺的小溪和田园屋舍，所有这一切构成了一幅宁静而又朴素的风景画。

R

S

salary

薪金，薪水

n. ['sæləri]

考试 TOEFL/IELTS/PTE
科目 reading

A more detailed salary analysis shows big differences between sectors of employment.

一份更详细的薪酬分析报告显示，不同就业领域之间存在着巨大差距。

sale

销售；销售额

n. [seɪl]

考试 KET/PET/IELTS/TOEFL/PTE
科目 all

The company reported booming sales figures.

这家公司发布了销售额迅速增长的消息。

satisfy

满意；使满意；使相信，使确信

vt. ['sætɪsfaɪ]

考试 KET/PET/IELTS/TOEFL/PTE
科目 all

He wanted to satisfy himself that he had given his best performance.

他想让自己确信他已经发挥到极致了。

sausage

香肠，腊肠

n. ['sɒsɪdʒ]

考试 KET/PET/IELTS/TOEFL/PTE
科目 all

The cook stuffed the chicken with sausage meat.

厨师往鸡里塞了香肠肉。

scandal

冒犯或引起反感的行为；丑行；丑闻；可耻的行为

n. [ˈskændl]

考试 TOEFL/IELTS/PTE
科目 reading

There has been no hint of scandal during his time in office.

他在任职期间没有任何丑闻。

scarf

围巾，头巾；领巾；领带

n. [skɑːf]

考试 KET/PET/IELTS/TOEFL/PTE
科目 all

To warm the air before you breathe it, use a scarf or mask.

在你呼吸之前，用围巾或者口罩使进入口腔的空气变暖和。

scientist

科学家

n. [ˈsaɪəntɪst]

考试 KET/PET/IELTS/TOEFL/PTE
科目 all

The scientist is an international leader in the field of mathematics.

这位科学家在数学这一领域处于国际领先地位。

score

分数；二十；配乐

n. [skɔː(r)]

考试 KET/PET/IELTS/TOEFL/PTE
科目 all

The film picked up awards for best director and best original score.

这部影片获得了 "最佳导演奖" 和 "最佳原创音乐奖"。

S

记分；得分

v. [skɔː(r)]

考试 KET/PET/IELTS/TOEFL/PTE
科目 all

Girls usually score highly in language exams.

在语言考试中，女生通常得高分。

scrape

刮，擦；挖坑；（使）发出刺耳的刮擦声

v. ［skreɪp］

考试 TOEFL/IELTS
科目 writing

The journey through the bush had caused John to tear his pajamas, and scrape his chin, knee and elbow.
在穿越灌木丛的路上，约翰的睡衣已经撕烂了，他的下颏、膝盖和肘臂都刮伤了。

screen

屏幕；屏风；帘

n. ［skriːn］

考试 KET/PET/IELTS/TOEFL/PTE
科目 all

They put a screen in front of me so I couldn't see what was going on.
他们在我面前竖了一面屏风，所以我看不到发生了什么事情。

掩蔽；包庇；筛选

vt. ［skriːn］

考试 KET/PET/IELTS/TOEFL/PTE
科目 all

Most of the road behind the hotel was screened by a block of flats.
宾馆后面的那条路大部分被一片公寓楼遮住了。

scrutiny

细察；调查

n. ［ˈskruːtəni］

考试 TOEFL/IELTS/PTE
科目 reading

Parliament operates an effective scrutiny system.
国会执行了一项有效的审查制度。

secretary

秘书；书记；部长，大臣

n. ［ˈsekrətri］

考试 KET/PET/IELTS/TOEFL/PTE
科目 all

The treasury secretary declined to comment.
财政部长拒绝做出评论。

security

安全；保证；证券

n. [sɪˈkjʊərəti]

考试 TOEFL/IELTS/PTE
科目 reading

If an alarm gives you that feeling of security, then it's worth carrying.

如果带着闹钟让你感到心里踏实，那就值得携带。

seek

寻找，探索；试图，企图

v. [siːk]

考试 KET/PET/IELTS/TOEFL/PTE
科目 all

Moscow is seeking to slow the growth of Russian inflation.

俄罗斯政府正力图遏制本国的通货膨胀。

seize

抓住，逮住；夺取；占领

vt. [siːz]

Police were reported to have seized all copies of this morning's edition of the newspaper.

据说警方已经将该报纸今天的早间版全部没收。

senior

年长的；地位较高的

adj. [ˈsiːniə(r)]

考试 KET/PET/IELTS/TOEFL/PTE
科目 all

I have ten years' experience at senior management level.

我有 10 年的高层管理经验。

（大学）四年级学生

n. [ˈsiːniə(r)]

考试 KET/PET/IELTS/TOEFL/PTE
科目 all

She is already a senior in the college hunting for the first job.

她已经是大学四年级学生，开始找工作了。

S

separate

分离的，分开的

adj. [ˈsepərət]

考试 KET/PET/IELTS/TOEFL/PTE
科目 all

Business bank accounts were kept separate from personal ones.

银行的商业账户和个人账户是分开管理的。

分离，分开

v. [ˈsepəreɪt]

考试 KET/PET/IELTS/TOEFL/PTE
科目 all

Those suffering from infectious diseases were separated from the other patients.

传染病患者同其他患者分隔开了。

servant

仆人；雇员，职员

n. [ˈsɜːvənt]

考试 KET/PET/IELTS/TOEFL/PTE
科目 all

Like any other public servants, police must respond to public demand.

和其他所有公务员一样，警察必须服务于公众的需求。

serve

端上；提供；服务；尽责；招待，侍候；符合，适用

v. [sɜːv]

考试 KET/PET/IELTS/TOEFL/PTE
科目 all

I wanted to work somewhere where I could serve the community.

我想找一个能够为公众服务的工作岗位。

service

服务；公共设施；维修，保养；工作，服务

n. [ˈsɜːvɪs]

考试 KET/PET/IELTS/TOEFL/PTE
科目 all

We offer excellent after-sales service on all our goods.

我们对所有商品提供优质的售后服务。

维修；提供服务

vt. ［ˈsɜːvɪs］

考试 KET/PET/IELTS/TOEFL/
PTE
科目 all
We need to have the car serviced.
我们得把车送去检修一下了。

shadowy

有阴影的；幽暗的；朦胧的

adj. ［ˈʃædəʊi］

考试 KET/PET/IELTS/TOEFL/
PTE
科目 all
Someone was waiting in the shadowy doorway.
有人守候在昏暗的门口。

sharp

锋利的；清晰的；急剧的；鲜明的

adj. ［ʃɑːp］

考试 KET/PET/IELTS/TOEFL/
PTE
科目 all
In sharp contrast to her mood, the clouds were breaking up to reveal a blue sky.
乌云渐渐散开，露出了蓝天，这和她的情绪形成了鲜明的对照。

（表示准时）……整

adv. ［ʃɑːp］

考试 KET/PET/IELTS/TOEFL/
PTE
科目 all
Please be here at eight o'clock sharp.
请八点整来到这里。

sharpen

削尖；使敏锐；（使）变得锋利，变得清晰

v. ［ˈʃɑːpən］

考试 TOEFL/IELTS
科目 writing
There is a need to sharpen the focus of the discussion.
有必要使讨论的焦点更加集中。

S

shatter

（使）破碎；粉碎，毁损

v. [ˈʃætə(r)]

考试 TOEFL/IELTS
科目 writing

He dropped the vase and it shattered into pieces on the floor.
他失手把花瓶掉在地板上摔碎了。

shiny

光亮的，有光泽的

adj. [ˈʃaɪni]

考试 KET/PET/IELTS/TOEFL/PTE
科目 all

His face was red and shiny.
他红光满面。

shipping

航运，装运

n. [ˈʃɪpɪŋ]

考试 KET/PET/IELTS/TOEFL/PTE
科目 all

The shipping company will be liable for damage.
运输公司将对损坏负责。

shiver

颤抖，哆嗦

vi. [ˈʃɪvə(r)]

考试 TOEFL/IELTS
科目 writing

He shivered at the thought of the cold, dark sea.
那寒冷黑暗的大海，他想想都发抖。

shock

震惊；休克

n. [ʃɒk]

考试 KET/PET/IELTS/TOEFL/PTE
科目 all

He has never recovered from the shock of your brother's death.
他从未从你哥哥去世的打击中恢复过来。

（使）震惊；使气愤；使厌恶

v. ［ʃɒk］

考试 KET/PET/IELTS/TOEFL/ PTE
科目 all

I was shocked to hear that he had resigned.
听到他辞职的消息，我深感意外。

shot

发射；投篮；镜头

n. ［ʃɒt］

考试 KET/PET/IELTS/TOEFL/ PTE
科目 all

Taylor scored with a low shot into the corner of the net.
泰勒一脚低射，把球射入网角。

shower

阵雨；淋浴

n. ［'ʃaʊə(r)］

考试 KET/PET/IELTS/TOEFL/ PTE
科目 all

We were caught in a heavy shower.
我们遇上了一阵大雨。

shuffle

洗牌；拖拽；坐立不安

v. ［'ʃʌfl］

考试 TOEFL/IELTS
科目 writing

Shuffle the cards and deal out seven to each player.
洗洗牌，然后给每人发七张。

silent

寂静的；沉默的

adj. ［'saɪlənt］

考试 KET/PET/IELTS/TOEFL/ PTE
科目 all

He spoke no English and was completely silent during the visit.
他不会说英语，参观过程中一言未发。

S

silver

银；银器；银币

n. [ˈsɪlvə(r)]

考试 KET/PET/IELTS/TOEFL/PTE
科目 all

This board was cast in bronze, not in silver.
这个牌匾是铜铸的，不是银制的。

镀银；使具有银色光泽

vt. [ˈsɪlvə(r)]

考试 KET/PET/IELTS/TOEFL/PTE
科目 all

Moonlight was silvering the countryside.
月光下的乡村泛着银光。

simple

简单的；单纯的，直率的；头脑简单的

adj. [ˈsɪmpl]

考试 KET/PET/IELTS/TOEFL/PTE
科目 all

I like my clothes to be simple but elegant.
我喜欢朴素雅致的衣服。

situate

使位于，使坐落在

vt. [ˈsɪtʃueɪt]

考试 TOEFL/IELTS
科目 writing

They are trying to decide where to situate the hospital.
他们正设法确定医院的修建地点。

skip

跳跃；遗漏

n. [skɪp]

考试 KET/PET/IELTS/TOEFL/PTE
科目 all

He read the lengthy report without a skip.
他从头到尾阅读了那份冗长的报告。

跳过；遗漏

v. ［skɪp］

考试 KET/PET/IELTS/TOEFL/ PTE
科目 all

If we skip a step or change the order we won't get the same results.

如果我们漏掉了一步，或者改变了顺序，得到的将是不同的结果。

skyrocket

猛涨，飞涨

vi. ［ˈskaɪrɒkɪt］

考试 TOEFL/IELTS
科目 writing

Production has dropped while prices and unemployment have skyrocketed.

在物价和失业率猛涨的同时，生产却下降了。

skyscraper

摩天大楼

n. ［ˈskaɪskreɪpə(r)］

考试 KET/PET/IELTS/TOEFL/ PTE
科目 all

He wants to build a skyscraper called the Dynamic Tower in Dubai.

他想在迪拜建造一幢名为"动力大楼"的摩天大楼。

slip

滑倒；错误

n. ［slɪp］

考试 KET/PET/IELTS/TOEFL/ PTE
科目 all

He recited the whole poem without making a single slip.

他一字不差地背诵了全诗。

S

滑倒；滑落，脱离；迅速放置；偷偷放

v. ［slɪp］

考试 KET/PET/IELTS/TOEFL/ PTE
科目 all

We are too close to allow success to slip through our fingers.

我们已经如此接近成功，不能听任它从指缝中溜走。

slipper

便鞋，拖鞋

n. [ˈslɪpə(r)]

考试 KET/PET/IELTS/TOEFL/PTE
科目 all

He kicked his slippers off and dropped on to the bed.
他踢掉了拖鞋，躺倒在床上。

smog

烟雾

n. [smɒg]

考试 KET/PET/IELTS/TOEFL/PTE
科目 all

Environmental degradation is now so severe that suffocating smog surrounds major highways and transportation arteries routinely.
如今，环境退化非常严重，以致很多交通要道经常受到浓雾的致命侵袭。

snail

蜗牛；行动缓慢的人

n. [sneɪl]

考试 KET/PET/IELTS/TOEFL/PTE
科目 all

The economy grew at a snail's pace in the first three months of this year.
今年第一季度经济增速缓慢。

soak

浸泡；淋湿；使湿透

v. [səʊk]

考试 TOEFL/IELTS
科目 writing

A sudden shower of rain soaked the spectators.
突如其来的一阵雨把观众淋湿了。

social

社会的；交际的

adj. [ˈsəʊʃl]

考试 KET/PET/IELTS/TOEFL/PTE
科目 all

Social events and training days are arranged for all the staff.
所有的员工都安排有联谊活动和培训。

soda

苏打汽水

n. [ˈsəʊdə]

考试 KET/PET/IELTS/TOEFL/PTE
科目 all

The military handed out some cookies and soda.
军方配给他们一些饼干和苏打汽水。

softly

柔软地；温柔地

adv. [ˈsɒftli]

考试 KET/PET/IELTS/TOEFL/PTE
科目 all

Use the eraser and softly erase parts of the line.
使用橡皮擦轻轻地擦掉部分线条。

solid

固体的；结实的，稳固的；可靠的

adj. [ˈsɒlɪd]

考试 KET/PET/IELTS/TOEFL/PTE
科目 all

A solid global recovery demands healthy and balanced growth in private demand.
稳固的全球经济复苏需要私人消费需求健康且均衡的增长。

固体

n. [ˈsɒlɪd]

考试 KET/PET/IELTS/TOEFL/PTE
科目 all

Solids turn to liquids at certain temperatures.
固体在一定的温度下会变为液体。

solve

解决；解答

v. [sɒlv]

考试 KET/PET/IELTS/TOEFL/PTE
科目 all

Attempts are being made to solve the problem of waste disposal.
正在想办法解决废物处理的问题。

S

soothe

安慰；使镇定

vt. ［suːð］

考试 TOEFL/IELTS/PTE
科目 reading

A nice cup of tea will soothe your nerves.
一杯好茶可以使你的心绪平静下来。

soul

灵魂，心灵，精神

n. ［səʊl］

考试 KET/PET/IELTS/TOEFL/
PTE
科目 all

The soft handwriting reflected a thoughtful soul and
insightful mind.
柔和的笔迹反映了一个有思想的心灵和富有洞察力的
头脑。

sow

播种，种；散布

v. ［saʊ］

考试 TOEFL/IELTS
科目 writing

The fields around had been sown with wheat.
近处的地里种上了小麦。

spaceship

宇宙飞船

n. ［ˈspeɪsʃɪp］

考试 KET/PET/IELTS/TOEFL/
PTE
科目 all

The spaceship made a safe landing on the moon.
宇宙飞船在月球上安全着陆了。

spark

火花，火星

n. ［spɑːk］

考试 TOEFL/IELTS/PTE
科目 reading

A shower of sparks flew up the chimney.
烟囱里飞出了无数火星。

specialize

专门研究；专攻

vi. [ˈspeʃəlaɪz]

考试 TOEFL/IELTS
科目 writing

The shop specializes in hand-made chocolates.
这家商店专营手工制作的巧克力。

specify

指定；详细说明

vt. [ˈspesɪfaɪ]

考试 TOEFL/IELTS
科目 writing

Remember to specify your size when ordering clothes.
订购服装时记着要详细说明你要的号码。

speculate

推测，推断；投机

v. [ˈspekjuleɪt]

考试 TOEFL/IELTS
科目 writing

Big farmers are moving in, not in order to farm, but in order to speculate with rising land prices.
大农场主正在不断涌进来，不是为了耕作，而是要利用不断上涨的地价进行投机。

spicy

辛辣的；香的；加香料的

adj. [ˈspaɪsi]

考试 KET/PET/IELTS/TOEFL/
PTE
科目 all

Sichuan was best known for its spicy food.
四川以辛辣的食物而知名。

S

spider

蜘蛛

n. [ˈspaɪdə(r)]

考试 KET/PET/IELTS/TOEFL/
PTE
科目 all

She stared in horror at the hairy black spider.
她恐惧地盯着那只毛茸茸的黑蜘蛛。

spirit

精神，心灵；情绪，心情

n. [ˈspɪrɪt]

考试 KET/PET/IELTS/TOEFL/PTE
科目 all

You must try and keep your spirits up.
你必须设法保持高昂的情绪。

spot

斑点；地点

n. [spɒt]

考试 KET/PET/IELTS/TOEFL/PTE
科目 all

He showed the police the exact spot where the accident happened.
他向警方指认了事故发生的确切地点。

认出，认清，发现；玷污，弄脏

vt. [spɒt]

考试 KET/PET/IELTS/TOEFL/PTE
科目 all

Neighbours spotted smoke coming out of the house.
邻居们发现有烟从这所房子里冒出来。

stability

稳定，安定

n. [stəˈbɪləti]

考试 TOEFL/IELTS/PTE
科目 reading

The government has taken measures to maintain the stability of prices.
政府已经采取了措施以确保物价稳定。

stake

木桩；赌注；股份；重大利益，重大利害关系

n. [steɪk]

考试 TOEFL/IELTS
科目 writing

She has personal stake in the success of the play.
这出戏成功与否对她个人有重大利害关系。

startle

惊吓，使吃惊

vt. ['stɑːtl]

考试 TOEFL/IELTS
科目 writing

He answered all the questions with a readiness that startled everyone present.

他敏捷地回答了所有问题，使在座的每个人为之震惊。

starve

（使）挨饿；渴望

v. [stɑːv]

考试 TOEFL/IELTS
科目 writing

She's starving herself to try to lose weight.

她试图通过节食来减肥。

statement

声明，陈述；报表

n. ['steɪtmənt]

考试 KET/PET/IELTS/TOEFL/
PTE
科目 all

The statement by the military denied any involvement in last night's attack.

军方发表声明称其与昨晚的袭击无任何关系。

steel

钢铁

n. [stiːl]

考试 KET/PET/IELTS/TOEFL/
PTE
科目 all

The company has interests in steel and other products.

这家公司在钢铁和其他产品领域都有投资。

stick

棍，棒；手杖

n. [stɪk]

考试 KET/PET/IELTS/TOEFL/
PTE
科目 all

The old lady leant on her stick as she talked.

老太太说话时拄着拐杖。

S

刺，戳，扎；粘贴

v. ［stɪk］

考试 KET/PET/IELTS/TOEFL/
PTE
科目 all

Her wet clothes were sticking to her body.

湿衣服粘在她身上。

sticky

黏的，黏性的；难办的，棘手的

adj. ［ˈstɪki］

考试 KET/PET/IELTS/TOEFL/
PTE
科目 all

Her research was going through a sticky patch.

她的研究工作正处于一个艰难的阶段。

stimulate

刺激，使兴奋；激励，鼓舞

vt. ［ˈstɪmjuleɪt］

考试 TOEFL/IELTS/PTE
科目 reading

I hoped my warning would stimulate her to greater efforts.

我希望我的告诫会促使她做出更大的努力。

stipulate

规定，约定

vt. ［ˈstɪpjuleɪt］

考试 TOEFL/IELTS
科目 writing

The job advertisement stipulates that the applicant must have three years' experience.

招聘广告明确要求应聘者必须有三年工作经验。

stir

搅拌，搅动；摇动；激动；轰动；煽动

v. ［stɜː(r)］

考试 KET/PET/IELTS/TOEFL/
PTE
科目 all

Whenever he's around, he always manages to stir up trouble.

什么时候只要有他在，他就总是挑起事来。

storage

贮藏（量）；保管；库房

n. [ˈstɔːrɪdʒ]

考试 KET/PET/IELTS/TOEFL/PTE
科目 all

The management accept full responsibility for loss of goods in storage.

管理部门接受仓库中货物损失的全部责任。

stove

炉子，火炉；厨房灶具，炉具

n. [stəʊv]

考试 KET/PET/IELTS/TOEFL/PTE
科目 all

Most people don't want to spend hours slaving over a hot stove.

人们大都不愿老围着热灶台转。

strategy

战略；策略

n. [ˈstrætədʒi]

考试 KET/PET/IELTS/TOEFL/PTE
科目 all

Each country needs to forge its own industrial development strategy.

每个国家都需要制定自己的工业发展战略。

straw

稻草；麦秆；吸管

n. [strɔː]

考试 KET/PET/IELTS/TOEFL/PTE
科目 all

He was leaning over the gate chewing on a straw.

他嘴里嚼着一根麦秆，靠在栅门上。

stream

小河，溪流；流；一股；一串

n. [striːm]

考试 KET/PET/IELTS/TOEFL/PTE
科目 all

Stream restoration projects create great sense of pride amongst residents.

河流恢复项目能建立居民强烈的自豪感。

S

流出，涌出

v. ［stri:m］

考试 KET/PET/IELTS/TOEFL/
PTE
科目 all

She came in, rain streaming from her clothes and hair.

她进来时，雨水顺着她的衣服和头发往下流。

strike

罢工

n. ［straɪk］

考试 KET/PET/IELTS/TOEFL/
PTE
科目 all

The strike has delivered a heavy blow to the management.

这场罢工给资方以一个沉重打击。

打，击；攻击；给……深刻印象

v. ［straɪk］

考试 KET/PET/IELTS/TOEFL/
PTE
科目 all

What strikes me as interesting is how much we judge other people by the clothes they wear.

让我觉得很有意思的是我们经常以衣取人。

striking

引人注目的；显著的

adj. ［ˈstraɪkɪŋ］

考试 KET/PET/IELTS/TOEFL/
PTE
科目 all

She bears a striking resemblance to her older sister.

她酷似她的姐姐。

structure

结构，构造；建筑物

n. ［ˈstrʌktʃə(r)］

考试 KET/PET/IELTS/TOEFL/
PTE
科目 all

The house was a handsome four-story brick structure.

这所房子是一幢造型美观的四层砖砌建筑物。

使形成体系，系统安排；建造

vt. ['strʌktʃə(r)]

考试 KET/PET/IELTS/TOEFL/PTE
科目 all

The exhibition is structured around the themes of work and leisure.

此次展览是围绕工作与休闲的主题来布置的。

stubborn

顽固的；难处理的

adj. ['stʌbən]

考试 TOEFL/IELTS/PTE
科目 reading

Commercial stain removers are usually a good choice for more stubborn stains.

较顽固的污渍选择商用污渍去除剂，这通常是个好办法。

stumble

绊跌，绊倒；踌躇

vi. ['stʌmbl]

考试 TOEFL/IELTS
科目 writing

We were stumbling around in the dark looking for a candle.

黑暗中，我们东跌西撞地找蜡烛。

submerge

放于水下；使沉没；浸没，淹没；湮没，湮灭

v. [səb'mɜːdʒ]

考试 TOEFL/IELTS
科目 writing

The fields had been submerged by flood water.

农田被洪水淹没了。

sudden

出乎意料的，突然的

adj. ['sʌdn]

考试 KET/PET/IELTS/TOEFL/PTE
科目 all

He believes the transition would happen slowly, rather than a sudden switch.

他认为，这个过渡会缓慢进行，而不会是一个突然的转变。

S

suggestion

建议；细微的迹象；联想

n. ［səˈdʒestʃən］

考试 KET/PET/IELTS/TOEFL/
PTE
科目 all

Most advertisements work through suggestion.
多数广告都是通过暗示发挥作用的。

summary

概括的；概要的

adj. ［ˈsʌməri］

考试 KET/PET/IELTS/TOEFL/
PTE
科目 all

I made a summary report for the records.
我对记录内容做了扼要报告。

总结，概括，概要

n. ［ˈsʌməri］

考试 KET/PET/IELTS/TOEFL/
PTE
科目 all

In summary, this was a disappointing performance.
总的来说，这场演出令人失望。

sunrise

日出，拂晓

n. ［ˈsʌnraɪz］

考试 KET/PET/IELTS/TOEFL/
PTE
科目 all

In general, at sunrise and sunset, lower clouds carry less colour than higher ones.
一般说来，在日出和日落的时候，较低的云层与较高的云层相比，其带来的色彩比较微弱。

sunset

日落，傍晚

n. ［ˈsʌnset］

考试 KET/PET/IELTS/TOEFL/
PTE
科目 all

Every evening at sunset the flag was lowered.
每天傍晚日落时都要降旗。

surpass

超越；超过，胜过

v. ［səˈpɑːs］

考试 TOEFL/IELTS/PTE
科目 reading

The young athlete's success has surpassed all expectations.
这名年轻运动员的成功远远超出了预期。

sustain

支持；维持；承担

vt. [sə'steɪn]

考试 TOEFL/IELTS/PTE
科目 reading

I am sustained by letters of support and what people say to me in ordinary daily life.

这些支持的信件和人们每天对我的鼓励一直支撑着我。

swan

天鹅

n. [swɒn]

考试 KET/PET/IELTS/TOEFL/PTE
科目 all

The swan is mostly silent through its life；it floats quietly on the water，unable to sing sweet songs like most other birds.

天鹅一生大多数时间是安静的，它静静地漂浮在水面上，无法像大多数其他鸟类一样唱出甜美的歌声。

sweep

扫除；连绵区域；范围；全胜

n. [swi:p]

考试 KET/PET/IELTS/TOEFL/PTE
科目 all

Her well-known book covers the long sweep of the country's history.

她的著作涵盖了该国漫长的历史。

扫除；猛拉；蜿蜒，呈斜坡延伸

v. [swi:p]

考试 KET/PET/IELTS/TOEFL/PTE
科目 all

The hotel gardens sweep down to the beach.

旅馆的花园呈缓坡一直延伸到海滩。

swell

使增强，使壮大；使隆起

v. [swel]

考试 TOEFL/IELTS
科目 writing

We are looking for more volunteers to swell the ranks.

我们期盼有更多的志愿者加入，以壮大队伍。

S

swing

摆动，摇动；旋转，转向；（使）突然转向，突然转身

v. [swɪŋ]

考试 KET/PET/IELTS/TOEFL/ PTE
科目 all

He swung the camera around to face the opposite direction.

他猛地将照相机转了个方向对着反方。

摆动；秋千

n. [swɪŋ]

考试 KET/PET/IELTS/TOEFL/ PTE
科目 all

Ian lit a cigarette and sat on the end of the table, taking a swing of one leg.

伊恩点燃了一支烟，坐在桌子的一端，一条腿晃来晃去。

symbol

符号；标志；象征

n. [ˈsɪmbl]

考试 KET/PET/IELTS/TOEFL/ PTE
科目 all

Helen became a symbol of new hope for the deaf and blind.

海伦作为一个标志给聋哑人和盲人带来了新的希望。

symbolize

象征；用符号表现

vt. [ˈsɪmbəlaɪz]

考试 TOEFL/IELTS
科目 writing

Light blue may symbolize hope, healing and a high level of spiritual awareness.

淡蓝色可能象征着希望、康复和高层次的精神意识。

symphony

交响乐；和声

n. [ˈsɪmfəni]

考试 KET/PET/IELTS/TOEFL/ PTE
科目 all

Brain growth is like a symphony, and all parts must be developing at the correct tempo.

大脑的发育就好比一首交响曲，每个部分都要合着正确的节拍运作。

T

---

tabulate

把……制成表

vt. [ˈtæbjuleɪt]

考试 TOEFL/IELTS
科目 writing

We are going to tabulate the findings of our survey.
我们打算把我们调查的结果列成表格。

---

talent

才能；天资；人才，天才

n. [ˈtælənt]

考试 KET/PET/IELTS/TOEFL/
PTE
科目 all

The player was given hardly any opportunities to show off his talents.
那位选手几乎没有得到什么机会展示自己的天赋。

---

tax

税（款）；负担

n. [tæks]

考试 KET/PET/IELTS/TOEFL/
PTE
科目 all

They are calling for large spending cuts and tax increases.
他们呼吁大幅削减开支并提高税收。

对……征税，使负重担

vt. [tæks]

考试 KET/PET/IELTS/TOEFL/
PTE
科目 all

His declared aim was to tax the rich.
他宣布他的目的是向富人征税。

taxation

税项；征税

n. [tækˈseɪʃn]

考试 KET/PET/IELTS/TOEFL/PTE
科目 all

Almost all the media discussion has been around taxation of the rich and fairness.

几乎所有的媒体讨论都围绕着对富人征税和社会公平。

tease

取笑，嘲笑，戏弄

v. [tiːz]

考试 TOEFL/IELTS
科目 writing

Don't tease others about their names.

不要拿别人的名字开玩笑。

temple

庙宇，神殿；太阳穴

n. [ˈtempl]

考试 KET/PET/IELTS/TOEFL/PTE
科目 all

She had black hair, greying at the temples.

她头发乌黑，但两鬓渐白。

temporary

暂时的，临时的

adj. [ˈtemprəri]

考试 KET/PET/IELTS/TOEFL/PTE
科目 all

The embassy refused to renew their temporary travel documents.

大使馆不同意延长他们临时旅行证件的有效期。

thrill

激动；震颤

n. [θrɪl]

考试 KET/PET/IELTS/TOEFL/PTE
科目 all

It gave me a big thrill to meet my favourite author in person.

能见到我最喜欢的作者本人使我感到兴奋不已。

使非常激动；使非常兴奋

vt. ［θrɪl］

考试 KET/PET/IELTS/TOEFL/ PTE
科目 all
The band has thrilled audiences all over the world.
该乐队使全世界的观众狂热痴迷。

thrive

繁荣，兴旺

vi. ［θraɪv］

考试 TOEFL/IELTS/PTE
科目 reading
Creative people are usually very determined and thrive on overcoming obstacles.
富有创造力的人一般都意志非常坚定，能不断克服困难，事业蒸蒸日上。

throat

咽喉，嗓子

n. ［θrəʊt］

考试 KET/PET/IELTS/TOEFL/ PTE
科目 all
He paused for a moment to clear his throat.
他停了下来，清了清嗓子。

thunder

雷，雷声；轰隆声

n. ［ˈθʌndə(r)］

考试 KET/PET/IELTS/TOEFL/ PTE
科目 all
The thunder of the sea on the rocks seemed to blank out other thoughts.
海水拍打礁石的咆哮声似乎要淹没一切思绪。

tilt

（使）倾斜

v. ［tɪlt］

考试 TOEFL/IELTS
科目 writing
She tilted her head back and looked up at me with a smile.
她仰起头，含笑看着我。

T

tiny

极小的，微小的

adj. ［ˈtaɪni］

考试 KET/PET/IELTS/TOEFL/PTE
科目 all

The crop represents a tiny fraction of U. S. production.
农作物仅占美国出产物极小的一部分。

tiptoe

用脚尖走

vi. ［ˈtɪptəʊ］

考试 TOEFL/IELTS
科目 writing

I tiptoed over to the window.
我踮着脚走到窗前。

tire

（使）疲倦；（使）厌倦

v. ［ˈtaɪə(r)］

考试 KET/PET/IELTS/TOEFL/PTE
科目 all

He has made a good recovery but still tires easily.
他已康复得不错，但仍然容易感到疲劳。

toast

烤面包；干杯

n. ［təʊst］

考试 KET/PET/IELTS/TOEFL/PTE
科目 all

He spread some strawberry jam on his toast.
他把草莓酱涂在烤面包片上。

toil

辛劳工作；艰难地行动

vi. ［tɔɪl］

考试 TOEFL/IELTS
科目 writing

Hundreds of men toiled for years at building the pyramid.
数以百计的人辛苦了许多年建造了这座金字塔。

toothache

牙痛

n. [ˈtuːθeɪk]

考试 KET/PET/IELTS/TOEFL/
PTE
科目 all

When you have a toothache, you should immediately call the dentist.

当你牙痛的时候要立即看牙医。

toothpaste

牙膏

n. [ˈtuːθpeɪst]

考试 KET/PET/IELTS/TOEFL/
PTE
科目 all

The most important ingredient to look for when choosing toothpaste is fluoride.

选择牙膏时，最需要看的成分是氟化物。

tough

坚韧的；强壮的；坚强的；粗暴的，固执的

adj. [tʌf]

考试 TOEFL/IELTS/PTE
科目 reading

Whoever wins the election is going to have a tough job getting the economy back on its feet.

不管谁赢得选举都将面对复苏经济的棘手任务。

towel

毛巾，手巾

n. [ˈtaʊəl]

考试 KET/PET/IELTS/TOEFL/
PTE
科目 all

If you want a towel, look in the linen closet.

如果你需要毛巾，到毛巾柜里找好了。

tower

高耸；超越

vi. [ˈtaʊə(r)]

考试 KET/PET/IELTS/TOEFL/
PTE
科目 all

At school, a girl may tower over most boys her age.

在学校里，一个女孩可能比她同龄的大多数男孩都要高出许多。

T

tradition

传统，惯例

n. ［trəˈdɪʃn］

考试 KET/PET/IELTS/TOEFL/PTE
科目 all

Each country has its own indigenous cultural tradition.
每个国家都有其自身的文化传统。

tramp

徒步远行；长途跋涉

v. ［træmp］

考试 TOEFL/IELTS
科目 writing

She spent all day yesterday tramping the streets, gathering evidence.
她昨天一整天都在街上四处奔走，搜集证据。

trample

踩伤；践踏；伤害

v. ［ˈtræmpl］

考试 TOEFL/IELTS
科目 writing

Diplomats denounced the leaders for trampling their citizens' civil rights.
外交官谴责这些领导人践踏其公民的公民权。

treasure

财宝，财富；珍品

n. ［ˈtreʒə(r)］

考试 KET/PET/IELTS/TOEFL/PTE
科目 all

His greatest treasure is his collection of rock records.
他最珍爱的宝贝是他收藏的摇滚唱片。

珍爱，珍惜

vt. ［ˈtreʒə(r)］

考试 KET/PET/IELTS/TOEFL/PTE
科目 all

She treasures her memories of those joyous days.
她珍视那段快乐时光的记忆。

treatment

待遇；治疗，疗法

n. ['triːtmənt]

考试 KET/PET/IELTS/TOEFL/
PTE
科目 all

His treatment was a combination of surgery, radiation and drugs.

对他的治疗是将手术、放射和药物治疗结合在一起。

trickle

(使) 滴流，(使) 细流

v. ['trɪkl]

考试 TOEFL/IELTS
科目 writing

Tears were trickling down her cheeks.

眼泪顺着她的面颊流了下来。

triple

三倍数

n. ['trɪpl]

考试 KET/PET/IELTS/TOEFL/
PTE
科目 all

Fifteen is the triple of five.

15 是 5 的三倍数。

三倍的；三部分的

adj. ['trɪpl]

考试 KET/PET/IELTS/TOEFL/
PTE
科目 all

The amount of alcohol in his blood was triple the legal maximum.

他血液中的酒精含量为法定最高限量的三倍。

成为三倍；使增至三倍

v. ['trɪpl]

考试 KET/PET/IELTS/TOEFL/
PTE
科目 all

Output should triple by next year.

到明年产量应增至三倍。

T

tube

管，管子；软管

n. ［tjuːb］

考试 KET/PET/IELTS/TOEFL/PTE
科目 all

He squeezed out the last bit of toothpaste from the tube.

他将软管里的最后一点牙膏挤了出来。

tuition

教学；学费

n. ［tjuˈɪʃn］

考试 TOEFL/IELTS/PTE
科目 reading

My uncle will pay my tuition and also provide for my living expenses.

我的伯父将支付我的学费并提供我的生活费。

U

ugly

丑陋的；险恶的

adj. [ˈʌgli]

考试 KET/PET/IELTS/TOEFL/
PTE
科目 all

There were ugly scenes in the streets last night as rioting continued.

昨晚暴乱持续之际，街上险象环生。

underline

画线于……之下；强调

vt. [ˌʌndəˈlaɪn]

考试 KET/PET/IELTS/TOEFL/
PTE
科目 all

The doctor underlined that drinking too much could cause liver problems.

医生强调饮酒过度会导致肝功能问题。

undertake

承担；同意，答应

vt. [ˌʌndəˈteɪk]

考试 TOEFL/IELTS/PTE
科目 reading

She undertook the arduous task of monitoring the elections.

她承担了监督选举的艰巨任务。

unfold

（使）展开，打开

v. [ʌnˈfəʊld]

考试 TOEFL/IELTS
科目 writing

He quickly unfolded the blankets and spread them on the mattress.

他迅速展开毯子，铺在床垫上。

uniform

制服，军服；队服；统一服装

n. [ˈjuːnɪfɔːm]

考试 KET/PET/IELTS/TOEFL/PTE
科目 all

She will probably take great pride in wearing school uniform.

她很可能会为穿上校服而感到非常自豪。

unlawful

不合法的，违法的

adj. [ʌnˈlɔːfl]

考试 TOEFL/IELTS/PTE
科目 reading

He was arrested for the unlawful possession of fire arms.

他因非法持有武器而被捕。

unlock

开……的锁；开启；发现，揭示

vt. [ˌʌnˈlɒk]

考试 KET/PET/IELTS/TOEFL/PTE
科目 all

Education and training is the key that will unlock our nation's potential.

教育和培训是发掘我们国家潜力的关键。

unpaid

未付的；不支付薪水的；义务的

adj. [ˌʌnˈpeɪd]

考试 KET/PET/IELTS/TOEFL/PTE
科目 all

The unpaid volunteers do the work because they love it.

这些义务工作的志愿者是因为他们喜欢这项工作才做的。

urban

城市的，都市的

adj. [ˈɜːbən]

考试 TOEFL/IELTS/PTE
科目 reading

The income of urban and rural residents has gone up steadily.

城乡居民收入稳步增长。

useless

无用的，无价值的

adj. [ˈjuːsləs]

考试 KET/PET/IELTS/TOEFL/ PTE
科目 all

Don't trifle away your time on such useless things.

不要把你的时间浪费在这种无益的事情上。

utter

说，表达

v. [ˈʌtə(r)]

考试 TOEFL/IELTS
科目 writing

She did not utter a word during lunch.

吃午餐时，她一言未发。

U

V

valley

山谷；流域

n. [ˈvæli]

考试 KET/PET/IELTS/TOEFL/PTE
科目 all

The valley is continuously watered by the melting snow from the mountains.
群山融化的雪水不断流经山谷。

victim

牺牲品，受害者；受骗者

n. [ˈvɪktɪm]

考试 TOEFL/IELTS/PTE
科目 reading

Infectious diseases are spreading among many of the flood victims.
传染病正在遭受洪灾的很多灾民中蔓延。

vigorous

有力的，精力充沛的

adj. [ˈvɪgərəs]

考试 TOEFL/IELTS/PTE
科目 reading

His calligraphy is vigorous and forceful.
他的书法苍劲有力。

virus

病毒

n. [ˈvaɪrəs]

考试 KET/PET/IELTS/TOEFL/PTE
科目 all

There is a virus going round the world.
世界上流行着一种病毒性疾病。

vocation

职业，工作；信心，使命感

n. [vəʊˈkeɪʃn]

考试 KET/PET/IELTS/TOEFL/
PTE
科目 all

She is a doctor with a strong sense of vocation.
她是一个具有强烈使命感的医生。

volunteer

志愿者；志愿兵；自告奋勇者

n. [ˌvɒlənˈtɪə(r)]

考试 TOEFL/IELTS/PTE
科目 reading

The volunteer for community service is doing a good job.
社区服务的义工做得很出色。

vouch

担保

vi. [vaʊtʃ]

考试 TOEFL/IELTS
科目 writing

I can vouch for her ability to work hard.
我保证她能够努力工作。

V

W

wade

蹚（水或淤泥等）；跋涉

v. [weɪd]

考试 TOEFL/IELTS
科目 writing

They waded the river at a shallow point.
他们在浅水处蹚过河。

waive

放弃；搁置

vt. [weɪv]

考试 TOEFL/IELTS
科目 writing

In view of the unusual circumstances, they agree to waive their requirement.
鉴于特殊情况，他们同意放弃他们的要求。

wander

漫游；迷路；走神

v. [ˈwɒndə(r)]

考试 TOEFL/IELTS
科目 writing

To keep their bees from wandering, beekeepers feed them sugar solutions.
为了防止蜜蜂迷路，养蜂人给它们喝糖水。

wardrobe

衣柜；全部服装；行头

n. [ˈwɔːdrəʊb]

考试 KET/PET/IELTS/TOEFL/
PTE
科目 all

Put the wardrobe in the corner opposite the door.
把衣柜放在对着门的那个角落里。

warn

警告；提醒注意；使警惕；发出警告

v. ［wɔːn］

考试 KET/PET/IELTS/TOEFL/ PTE
科目 all

The farmer warned us off his land when we tried to camp there.

当我们想在那里露营时，农场主警告我们不得靠近他的土地。

The guidebook warns against walking alone at night.

这本指南告诫夜间不要单独行走。

warning

警告，告诫

n. ［ˈwɔːnɪŋ］

考试 KET/PET/IELTS/TOEFL/ PTE
科目 all

The bridge collapsed without any warning.

那座桥在没有任何先兆的情况下坍塌了。

wave

波浪；风潮；挥手；波

n. ［weɪv］

考试 KET/PET/IELTS/TOEFL/ PTE
科目 all

She declined the offer with a wave of her hand.

她摆摆手谢绝了这一提议。

挥手；挥手示意；挥舞，挥动；飘动，摇晃

v. ［weɪv］

考试 KET/PET/IELTS/TOEFL/ PTE
科目 all

I showed my pass to the security guard and he waved me through.

我向保安出示了通行证，他挥手让我通过。

W

weld

焊接；使紧密结合，使连成整体

v. ［weld］

考试 TOEFL/IELTS
科目 writing

All the parts of the sculpture have to be welded together.

这件雕塑的所有部件都必须焊接在一起。

whale

鲸；庞然大物

n. ［weɪl］

考试 KET/PET/IELTS/TOEFL/PTE
科目 all

Many coastal cities offer deep-sea fishing, whale watching and harbour cruises.

许多滨海城市会组织深海垂钓、观赏鲸鱼和海港巡游活动。

wheat

小麦

n. ［wiːt］

考试 KET/PET/IELTS/TOEFL/PTE
科目 all

By cereals we mean wheat, oats, rye, barley, and all that.

谈到谷物，我们指的是小麦、燕麦、黑麦、大麦之类的东西。

wheel

轮，车轮

n. ［wiːl］

考试 KET/PET/IELTS/TOEFL/PTE
科目 all

He braked suddenly, causing the front of wheels to skid.

他猛然刹车，使得前车轮打滑了。

width

宽阔，宽度

n. ［wɪdθ］

考试 KET/PET/IELTS/TOEFL/PTE
科目 all

The carpet is available in different widths.

这款地毯有各种宽度可供选择。

wither

(使）枯萎，凋谢；萎缩；（尤指渐渐）破灭，消失

v. [ˈwɪðə(r)]

考试 TOEFL/IELTS
科目 writing

The grass had withered in the warm sun.

这些草在温暖的阳光下枯萎了。

withhold

拒绝给；抑制

vt. [wɪðˈhəʊld]

考试 TOEFL/IELTS
科目 writing

She was accused of withholding information from the police.

她被指控对警方知情不报。

wring

拧，挤，扭；榨

vt. [rɪŋ]

考试 TOEFL/IELTS
科目 writing

Remember to wring your swimsuit out after you swim.

记住游泳过后要把泳衣拧干。

W